A Tale of
Two Funerals

Also by Dr. Alan Wolfelt

Creating Meaningful Funeral Ceremonies:
A Guide for Families

Creating Meaningful Funeral Experiences:
A Guide for Caregivers

Educating Families You Serve About the WHY of the Funeral:
A Guide for Funeral Home Staff

Finding the Words: How to Talk with Children
and Teens about Death, Suicide, Homicide, Funerals,
Cremation, and other End-of-Life Matters

Funeral Home Customer Service A-Z:
Creating Exceptional Experiences for Today's Families

The Pocket Consultant for Funeral Service:
Customer Service A-Z

A Tale of
Two Funerals

the THROW RUG
and the TAPESTRY

ALAN D. WOLFELT, PH.D.

Companion
PRESS

An imprint of the Center for Loss and Life Transition
Fort Collins, Colorado

Companion Press is an imprint of the Center for Loss and Life Transition, 3735 Broken Bow Road, Fort Collins, Colorado, 80526.

26 25 24 23 22 21 20 19 18 17   5 4 3 2 1

ISBN 978-1-61722-246-7

*"There are two great days in a person's life—
the day we are born and the day we discover why."*

— William Barclay

To all those for whom the creation of
meaningful funerals is a "why."

I believe that one of my "whys" is to help my fellow
human beings understand the value of meaningful
funeral experiences. My hope is that this book assists
you in your efforts to help families create funerals that
inspire them to say, "Now that was a great funeral."

And to my friend and colleague Dan Densow.
His knowledge and generosity in reviewing
drafts of these chapters were invaluable.

Companion
P R E S S

Companion Press is dedicated to the education and support
of both the bereaved and bereavement caregivers.
We believe that those who companion the bereaved by walking
with them as they journey in grief have a wondrous opportunity:
to help others embrace and grow through grief—and to lead fuller,
more deeply lived lives themselves because of this important ministry.

For a complete catalog and
ordering information, write, call, or visit:

Companion Press
The Center for Loss and Life Transition
3735 Broken Bow Road
Fort Collins, CO 80526
970.226.6050
www.centerforloss.com

Contents

Introduction

The phone call woke John Knight at three a.m. A funeral director for forty years, John was no stranger to wee-hour awakenings. Like its more celebrated twin—birth—death did not keep business hours.

John sat up, lifted the dedicated cell phone his company used for after-hours calls, silenced its ringtone, and stepped into his home office across the hall. No sense disturbing his sleeping wife any more than necessary.

"Hello. Knight & Day Funeral Home," he said. "How may I help you?" He moved to the window. Rain fell steadily, and in the distance, lightning flashed. The thunderstorm that the TV weatherperson had promised was beginning to roll in. As he spoke, he left the office lights off so he could better see the storm; such overnight displays were relatively rare in Colorado.

"It's my mother," said a woman's voice, thick with emotion. "We've had her at our house, and hospice has been helping take care of her...but... the rain woke me up, and I just went in to check on her...and... she's gone. I didn't know if I should call the hospice people, or you, or...." The woman spoke rapidly and emotionally; she was in distress.

"Oh, I'm so sorry," said John Knight, his gentle, genuine voice conveying both compassion and competence. "I will be happy to help you. It sounds like your mother had been ill?"

"Yes," said the woman. "Very sick. She had pancreatic cancer. But she was eighty-two…" The woman broke into a sob. "I'm sorry," she managed to say. "It's the middle of the night, and I don't know what I'm doing…"

"No, no need to apologize," assured John Knight. "It's always hard, even when it is expected." He sensed that before they began to talk about what came next, the woman wanted to tell him more about what had happened. "Pancreatic cancer can be so horrible," he added.

His intuition was right. The woman seemed to calm as she told him about her mother's diagnosis just months ago and her rapidly declining health ever since. Even though it was three in the morning and John had a long Monday ahead of him, he listened attentively as she spoke. He was owner of Knight & Day, the family-run funeral home his great-grandfather had opened nearly a hundred years ago, but he still took his turn in the on-call rotation. Many funeral homes had long since begun using removal services for such after-hours calls, but not John's. When it came to helping grieving families, Knight & Day meant night and day, as he always acknowledged to his staff whenever he thanked them for their above-and-beyond customer service.

"What is your mother's name?" asked John when the timing was right. He took care not to lapse into past tense, knowing it was too soon. Jennifer knew her mother was dead, but she did not *know* it yet.

"I'm sorry; her name is Carol Williams," said the woman. "I'm Jennifer Jones."

"Jennifer, we will take good care of your mother and your family," assured John Knight. As if to seal his promise, a loud clap of thunder boomed in the background.

John confirmed that Jennifer was her mother's executor, then explained to her that she should call the hospice to have their staff visit and make the official pronouncement of death. Next, he and one of his staff would come to take her mother to the funeral home. He asked Jennifer if she and her family would like to spend some time with Carol at home, or if Jennifer would prefer that he come as soon as possible.

"Oh...I don't know!" worried Jennifer. "I haven't done this before. My mother handled everything when my dad died..." She paused for a moment. Instead of jumping in, John gave her time to formulate her next question. "My younger son and husband are here," she continued. "Should I wake them?"

John hesitated. He knew that this was just the first of a myriad important decisions Jennifer would be making about Carol's funeral and disposition in the next several days. He and Knight & Day's entire staff were there to help her, but there was a fine line between guiding families toward healing choices and telling them what to do. So instead of answering her question, he asked one instead.

"Do you think your husband and son might be upset if they woke up and your mother was already gone from the house?" he asked. "Or if they were to awaken when I was there?"

"Ohhh," said Jennifer. "Yes. Yes, I don't think that would be good. I should go talk to them now. They might want to see her as she is, here in this house, one last time. And I should also call my brother before the next steps get taken."

"All right," said John Knight. "How about if we come at 5:30 a.m.? That will allow time for the hospice staff to visit and give you and your family a couple of hours to spend with your mother and to make phone calls before we arrive." Outside, the storm was growing more intense. The wind had picked up, and he could now hear the rain lashing and rattling the windows.

"OK," said Jennifer. "Yes. OK. 5:30. This is so surreal…"

After taking down Jennifer's address, John assured her that she should call him back as many times as she needed to between now and 5:30 if she had questions or concerns.

"I will see you in two hours," said John Knight. "And after we arrive, we will help you every step of the way. Do not worry."

John pressed the "end call" button on the cell phone and looked out at the storm. Lightning flashed, and thunder boomed. He might as well stay up, he thought. He wouldn't be able to fall back asleep with all this ruckus, anyway. Besides, ever since he was a boy, he'd always liked thunderstorms, but he rarely took the time to enjoy them. He'd sit here for a while and watch the show, and then he'd shower, dress, eat a bite of breakfast, and head out.

He'd also need to call one of his funeral directors soon, so they'd be ready to accompany him to the Williams' home for the removal. John Knight liked his staff. He found great reward in helping at-need families, but he also truly enjoyed spending time with his employees. They were good people.

John knew he would call one of two funeral directors for assistance this morning. Both were skilled. Sam Standard, one of John's nephews, had been with Knight & Day for what, twenty-nine years now? Sam was kind, patient, competent, and always willing to help. Families trusted him. Sam's younger colleague, Grace Gatekeeper, was the other option. She'd been in funeral service for just four years, but what enthusiasm! She was always coming up with crazy new ideas. Grace had just started handling arrangements by herself in the last year, and some of her funerals had been creating a buzz in their midsized suburban community of Collinsville—in a good way. Several families had raved about her.

John opened the window so he could smell the rain. It always reminded him of his childhood. But the wind gusted too fiercely, so John leaned forward to close it again. In that moment the on-call cell phone slipped from his hands. It skittered across the windowsill and through a small tear in the window screen that John had been meaning to repair. He watched helplessly as the phone plopped onto the ground below the roof overhang outside the main-floor window.

Never one to panic, John headed out of his office. He'd simply retrieve the phone before it got too wet. He'd reached his office door when *Crack!*—a blinding, oddly green flash of lightning lit the world indoors and out. The thunder seemed simultaneous with the flash of light. He jumped. That was a close one!

John Knight slipped on his rain jacket and boots. He grabbed a flashlight and, as he stepped through the front door, fought the wind and rain as he walked partway around the house to the office window. He found the cell phone and pocketed it, then hurried back inside. He'd never hear the end of it if his wife caught him outside in a lightning storm.

Back in the dry warmth of his foyer, John wiped his boots on the throw rug and swiped the cell phone on. He was worried it might have been damaged by the fall from the window or the rain and the lightning. But it powered up just fine, though he noticed that the screen's backlighting seemed to glow a little greener than it had before. He took off his boots and hung his coat on the wall hook next to the beautiful tapestry he had inherited from his grandparents and their parents before them—a family heirloom. Then he shuffled back down the hallway to his bedroom. It was time to get ready to go help the Williams family.

Little did John Knight know, but he and Knight & Day Funeral Home had just entered another dimension—a dimension of sound and sight, a dimension of mind and heart. In that nighttime that marked the border between life and death, a mysterious bolt of lightning had moved them into a land of both shadow and substance, of things and ideas. They had crossed over into a realm of two parallel universes, where Carol Williams' funeral would play out simultaneously under the direction of Sam Standard in one universe and Grace Gatekeeper in the other.

Lucky us. We are fortunate to be able to observe as the same person's funeral happens twice. How will the funerals be similar? How will they be different? Let's watch and learn together.

CHAPTER 1

Meet the Directors

EDITOR'S NOTE:

*This chapter and many that follow run Sam Standard's
and Grace Gatekeeper's versions of the funeral side by side.
This helps emphasize that the two funerals are happening
simultaneously. It also allows us to see at-a-glance what Sam
and Grace are doing differently at any given moment.
However, I recommend that in each chapter you first read
Sam's story, which appears on the left-hand pages,
all the way through then read Grace's. You will also notice
that I've highlighted small sections of text here and there
throughout the two storylines. These are the key moments that
differentiate Sam's funeral direction from Grace's. Feel free to add
your own highlighting, underlining, and notes in the margins.*

When Sam Standard's phone played its harp music at 4:30 a.m.—his kids assumed the ringtone was ironic, but Sam actually liked it—he was already awake. A loud clap of thunder had jolted him from a dream about fishing. He'd just hooked a lake trout—a big one, because it had nearly yanked the fishing rod from his hands. Sam rarely found free time for his favorite hobby. Now, awake and reaching for his phone, he felt a pang of disappointment that he didn't even get to land a dream trout.

On the other end of the line, Sam's boss, John Knight, told him that an elderly woman with cancer had died at her daughter's home. "I've arranged to pick her up 5:30," said John. "I'll swing by and get you on the way."

"Sure thing," said Sam. "See you soon."

Sam, John Knight's nephew, had worked for Knight & Day Funeral Home for his entire career in funeral service. In fact, his thirty-year anniversary date was next month. As he dressed, Sam found himself wondering absently how many death calls he'd taken in three decades. Let's see…a hundred times a year, on average…so, more than 3,000, almost certainly. That was a lot of dead people—and also a lot of families he'd felt privileged to help through their worst days. The feeling was mutual; many of them asked for him by name whenever someone they loved died.

Sam's wife, Becky, had already started a pot of coffee by the time he got to the kitchen. "Ahhhh…," he said, inhaling deeply. "Liquid energy! Thanks, honey."

With a start, Sam realized that if his thirtieth anniversary with Knight & Day was coming up soon, that meant his thirtieth wedding anniversary was fast-approaching, too. He and Becky had been married at St. Paul's Lutheran—the same church they

GRACE GATEKEEPER—the young, enthusiastic shaker-upper

Grace Gatekeeper may have been the go-go-go type when she was awake, but she slept like, well, the dead. It took three different alarms to get her up on time for work every morning. Fortunately, before she'd gone to bed the night before, she'd docked her cell phone in the speaker/alarm clock on her nightstand and turned the volume on high. So John Knight's 4:30 a.m. phone call not only blasted *her* out of bed, it also brought her roommate, Jason, running into her room in fear that something must be wrong.

"It's OK," she told Jason after hanging up with Mr. Knight. "Just a death call. Go back to bed."

Jason clapped his hands to his eyes in exasperation and left Grace's room. She knew Jason didn't "get" her choice of career. He wasn't the only one. Most of her twenty-something friends thought she was crazy.

"I *am* crazy," she mumbled to herself as she fished in her closet for something to wear. Dark dress slacks were suitable for removals. Maybe that dark top with the subtle dot pattern. Grace always wanted to convey respect, but she also liked a bit of energy in her outfits.

"Why *am* I doing this again?" she asked her cat, Winston, who still snoozed on her pillow. In response, her mind instantly conjured her mother.

After ten years of treatment and relapses, Grace's mom had finally succumbed to breast cancer when Grace was a junior in high school. And what do high-school juniors have to focus on (besides clothes, music, and dating)? Careers. Colleges. Before her mom died, Grace had no idea what she wanted to do. But after, Grace found herself oddly drawn to the rituals of the visitation, the ceremony, the committal service, and all the other funeral parts and pieces. Plus, the funeral home staff was so *present* to her. They weren't afraid to talk about what still attended most Sundays—soon after he finished mortuary school. What was the thirtieth anniversary gift again? Diamonds? Becky, he knew, would rather have a trip to Diamond Head on Oahu. Unfortunately, neither was probably in the cards. Maybe they could spend a weekend in Colorado's Rocky Mountains, not far from their home. Diamond Lake Trail near Nederland was beautiful…

"Day shift today?" Sam asked Becky. As an ICU nurse, she sometimes worked erratic hours, too, though rarely more than forty hours a week. She also understood death and the call to help people.

"Yep," said Becky. "Then I'm headed to the grocery store. Cameron and Lucy will be here tomorrow, remember?"

"Oh, right," said Sam. Cameron was their son, twenty-five years old and—finally—gainfully employed. He and his girlfriend, Lucy, would be visiting for the weekend. Sam hoped he'd be able to spend some time with them. "What about Jess?"

Jess was their daughter, a free-spirited philosophy major who'd quit college to "decide who she wanted to be." Meanwhile, she waitressed and shared a house in Denver with a motley crew of millennials.

"I didn't hear back from her," said Becky. "Maybe we'll see her; maybe we won't."

Sam kissed Becky good-bye and made his way to the front door, where he would watch for John Knight to pull up in the funeral home van. But on the way, he stopped for a moment to really look at the family photo gallery in the hallway, which he usually walked right by without noticing.

There was Cameron as a toddler, then in his baseball uniform, happened to her mother. They didn't look away when she started to cry. They understood death. The grieving Grace found herself wanting to understand death, too, and to help people as the funeral home staff did.

So despite her dad's trepidation, Grace declared she was going to community college for a two-year mortuary science degree. And she did. To celebrate after graduation, and in memory of her mother, she had a small angel tattooed on her chest near her heart.

Now, age twenty-six and the junior-most funeral director at Knight & Day, Grace had become all too aware of how hard funeral home employees worked. The hours were long. Grace couldn't stay out all night like some of her friends did. It was also all but impossible to find time for her other passions—books, vintage clothing, and travel.

Plus, Grace didn't always agree with the status quo at Knight & Day. In funeral service, "the way we've always done it" was sometimes a good thing and sometimes not so good, she'd observed.

Now that she had a few years as a funeral assistant and one year as a full-fledged funeral director under her belt, Grace found that she had lots of ideas. She didn't just want to help families cope and get by; she wanted to help them create funerals that were unique and unforgettable!

Why couldn't funerals be more like weddings? A lot of Grace's friends were getting married lately. In fact, her best friend, Molly, was getting married soon, and Grace would be a bridesmaid. Grace saw all the time the money and loving attention that were lavished on weddings. Shouldn't funerals be the same way, she figured? Aren't they just as important?

Grace remembered a talk she'd heard a funeral service innovator give at and later, rock-climbing. There was Jess after she'd lost her front teeth and, in high school, picking beans at the community garden. There were Sam and Becky on their wedding day. There were the four of them at Disney World—the one big trip he could remember taking as a family. There were Sam's parents at their fiftieth anniversary party— his father now dead and his mother alone in a senior high-rise.

Sam's mother was the same age as Carol Williams, it occurred to him. He really should find time to call her today, maybe even surprise her by bringing her lunch.

Sam heard the thrum of the funeral home van's engine in the driveway and stepped out into the dawning light to join John Knight. It was time to meet the Williams family and care for Carol Williams.

a recent funeral service convention. "The customer is rapidly changing," he'd warned. "And funeral service has to change, too—or you might as well put a sign in the front yard that says, 'Slowing Going Out of Business.'" Fortunately, John Knight was open-minded. He wanted to hear Grace's ideas. In fact, he looked to Grace to help Knight & Day adapt and thrive.

As Grace brushed her teeth, she raised her eyebrow at her reflection in the mirror. "Well?" her expression challenged. "Are you gonna go create an unforgettable funeral for the Williams family or not?"

She bounded out to the waiting funeral home van. Only after John Knight had handed her a tissue did she realize she'd neglected to wipe the toothpaste from her lips.

QUESTIONS FOR REFLECTION

1. At first glance, how are you similar to and different from Sam Standard and Grace Gatekeeper, both personally and professionally?

2. How are the funeral directors you have met or worked with similar to or different from Sam Standard and Grace Gatekeeper?

3. Why did you choose/are you choosing to be a funeral director? How have your motivations evolved since you first made the decision?

4. What do you believe is the role of funeral homes in your community and why?

5. Describe the worst funeral you have ever directed or attended. Why was it so ineffective?

6. Describe the best funeral you have ever directed or attended. Why was it so memorable and effective?

CHAPTER 2

The Transfer

As promised, Sam and John Knight pulled up at at the Williams' family home at 5:30 a.m. sharp. The fierce thunderstorm had subsided, and the rising sun pinked the clouds to the east.

Leaving the gurney and slide board in the Knight & Day funeral home van, Sam and John walked to the front door, where John knocked gently. On the short ride over, John had shared with Sam, his nephew and longtime employee, what the homeowner, Jennifer Jones, had told him about the woman who died—Jennifer's mother, Carol Williams, age eighty-two, pancreatic cancer.

"You must be Jennifer," said John Knight when a bleary-eyed woman answered the door. "I'm John Knight, and this is Sam Standard, my nephew and our most experienced funeral director."

"Oh. You're the funeral home people!" Jennifer said. She smiled ruefully and shook her head. "I didn't realize it was already morning. We've been sitting with Mom, but I guess it's time for her to go."

"There's no rush," assured Sam. "Maybe we could come inside and talk a little about the funeral? We also have paperwork to fill out, so there's no hurry."

Jennifer invited the men into her kitchen, where she offered them a cup of coffee. Jennifer's husband, Clark, soon joined them, and the foursome sipped coffee as the talk turned to pancreatic cancer.

"It's a terrible disease," agreed John. "As you can imagine, we meet many families who have gone through it. I'm sorry your mother had to suffer."

Jennifer wiped her eyes and nodded.

When Grace leaned in to knock on the Williams' family's door, she stopped herself mid-lean. "Tell me again what you know about Carol Williams?" she asked her boss, John Knight.

"Only that she is eighty-two and had pancreatic cancer," said John. "Her health declined rapidly, and Home Hospice has been helping take care of her here at her daughter Jennifer Jones' house."

"Got it," said Grace and knocked.

"Hi, Mrs. Jones," said Grace when a bleary-eyed woman answered the door. "My name is Grace. I'm with Knight & Day Funeral Home. And this is John Knight, the funeral home's owner. We're here to meet your mother and help you and your family."

"Oh!" Jennifer said. She smiled ruefully and shook her head. "I didn't realize it was already morning. We've been sitting with Mom, but I guess it's time for her to go."

"Not yet!" said Grace. "We all have to get to know each other a bit first. May we come in?"

Jennifer invited Grace and John into her kitchen, where she offered them a cup of coffee.

"I would love some coffee," said Grace, "but would it be OK with you if we visited your mother for a minute first?"

"Oh, of course," said Jennifer. "She's upstairs."

Grace and John followed Jennifer up the carpeted stairs and into the first bedroom on the right. "Here she is," said Jennifer, fondly smoothing back her mother's silvery hair. "Of course, she's much thinner now than she was a few months ago, before the cancer—too thin."

"You wouldn't know it to look at her now, but Carol was a real pistol," said Jennifer's husband, Clark, who had sidled into the room and placed

"You wouldn't know it to look at her now, but Carol was a real pistol," said Clark. "That cancer took the wind out of her sails in no time."

"And she was eighty-two," sighed Jennifer. "I guess we have to be grateful we had her as long as we did. Many people don't get to live so long."

"That's true," said Sam, looking Jennifer in the eye. "But it's never easy when it's someone we love, no matter how old they are. My mother is the same age, and I know that I'm going to be a mess when she dies."

Sam's empathy set Jennifer crying again. She stood to grab a tissue from the box on the counter and refill their coffee mugs.

"So tell me how this works," said Jennifer, blowing her nose and sitting down again. "I haven't done this before."

"We're here to make everything as easy as possible for you in the coming days," said Sam. "I'll be handling your mother's funeral arrangements, which means I'll be your main contact."

"Though everyone at Knight & Day is there to help as well," added John Knight.

"Do you know what kind of funeral your mother wanted?" asked Sam. "Don't worry—we're not going to try to make all the arrangements right this minute—we'll have a separate meeting tomorrow to go over all the details—but it would help to know generally what you have in mind. Did she have a funeral plan?"

"Well, my dad is buried at Collinsville Cemetery," said Jennifer, "so we'll put Mom next to him. Oh my gosh, I bet he's so happy to see her… No, she didn't have a formal plan—just a few things we'd talked about since she got sick."

"Perfect," said Sam, jotting down notes on the form. "And did his hands on his wife's shoulders.

Grace approached the bed and smiled down on Carol Williams. "Hello, Carol," said Grace, touching the old woman's hand. "I'm sorry I didn't get to meet you before now, but I promise I'll be taking good care of you and your family."

"Do you think she can hear you?" asked Jennifer, puzzled.

Grace smiled. "I think it's possible. But either way, I want her—and you— to know that being a funeral director isn't just my job. It's my passion. Every person who has died and every family I help is unique and special to me."

The foursome returned to the kitchen and sat down for a cup of coffee.

"You're awfully young to be doing this kind of work, aren't you?" Jennifer asked Grace. "You can't be much older than my sons."

"I've been working at Knight & Day for a few years already," said Grace. "Ever since my own mom died, I knew it was what I wanted to do."

"Grace is a wonderful funeral director," smiled John Knight. "You are in exceptional hands."

"On your mom's nightstand, I noticed the photos of your mom in her garden," said Grace. "Did she have a green thumb?"

"Oh yes, she always loved her garden!" said Jennifer. "Especially her dahlias. They were her favorite."

"And you said she was a real pistol, Mr. Jones," said Grace. "What was she like?"

Clark laughed. "Oh, she taught journalism for many years at the college. She was also a darned good bowler."

"I bet she was a fun grandma," said Grace.

she and your father attend a church where the funeral will be held?"

"Well," said Clark, "Carol's husband's was at the Episcopal church. Your mom's funeral will be there too, babe, right?"

"I guess so," shrugged Jennifer, "though Mom hasn't gone to church for a long time. Mostly what she kept saying is that we shouldn't go to any trouble. Mom always took care of everyone else, you see," she said, turning to Sam and John. "She didn't like the idea of us having to worry about her. It was hard enough for her that we had to take care of her the last few months."

"It sounds like she was a wonderful mother," said Sam. His gentle voice was sincere.

Jennifer's face crumpled and her shoulders shook. "Does everyone cry this much?" she sobbed.

"Just our favorites," said John.

Soon it was time to head upstairs. Sam and John carefully placed Carol Williams' body on the gurney and pulled the blanket they'd brought up to her shoulders. Jennifer and Clark followed as Sam and John wheeled it outside and slid Mrs. Williams into the funeral home van.

"We'll take good care of her," Sam assured Jennifer, confirming that they would be preparing Carol's body for viewing. "And I'll see you tomorrow for the arrangement conference. Here's my card with my cell phone number. Please call me whenever you have a question or concern, night or day. That's what I'm here for."

In the rearview mirror, John Knight could see Jennifer and Clark standing arm in arm in the driveway as the van pulled away.

"Nice family," commented Sam.

"Yes indeed," said John Knight. "Good people."

"Yes, she was," said Jennifer, who was crying again. "My kids and my brother's kids are going to miss her so much."

"We know you're probably very tired," said John Knight after a moment. "You'll be meeting with Grace tomorrow to go over all the arrangements."

"Yes!" said Grace brightly, as if shaking herself from a daydream. "I'm sure you have people to call and other things to take care of today, and I hope you can get some rest. Would you like a little more time with your mother before we leave?"

Jennifer and Clark returned upstairs, and a few minutes later, Grace and John followed. Grace invited Jennifer and Clark to help gently move Carol's body onto the gurney, then suggested that Jennifer tuck her mother in with the quilt they'd brought.

Outside, as they approached the van, Grace studied Jennifer's distraught face. "Do you want to ride with her to the funeral home?" Grace offered impulsively. "There's room for you up front with us. But if you don't want to, you'll be able to see her again tomorrow."

"Thanks, but I think I'll stay here," Jennifer said. She leaned down and kissed her mother's cheek. "I'll see you tomorrow," she whispered.

Grace gave Jennifer a quick hug. "I'm looking forward to helping you plan an amazing funeral for such an amazing person," Grace told her. "I'll check in with you later today about some details, and we'll meet tomorrow. Maybe your brother can come tomorrow as well?"

As the van pulled away, John Knight looked over at Grace, whose thumbs danced in hyper-speed on her phone. "Awful early to be texting, isn't it?" he chuckled.

"Not texting," said Grace. "Just getting down ideas for Mrs. Williams' funeral so I don't forget them!"

1. First, what is your general impression of how Sam Standard handled the transfer? What about your general impression of Grace Gatekeeper's version?

2. Sam says that his job is to make things as easy for the family as possible. Do you agree or disagree with this statement? Why or why not?

3. In what ways did Grace Gatekeeper's choice to ask to see Carol Williams right away influence the remainder of the transfer meeting with the family?

4. Grace asks more questions about Carol Williams than Sam does. Why do you think she does this?

5. Grace asks the family if they would like a little more time with their mother before they take her to the funeral home. Why might this be a good idea?

6. As Carol Williams' body is transferred to the gurney, Grace invites Jennifer to tuck her mother in. How does this affect the rest of the interaction in this chapter?

CHAPTER 3

The Preparation

Back at his desk at Knight & Day Funeral Home after the transfer of Carol Williams, Sam began entering information about Mrs. Williams into his computer.

Carol's daughter, Jennifer, had mentioned that Carol's husband had predeceased her. Luckily, Sam was able to locate Henry Williams' obituary and paperwork. Though Henry had died twelve years ago, the existing documentation still provided many of the details Sam would need to fill out Carol's many forms. There was no sense taking up any more of Carol's children's time than necessary for paperwork during the arrangement conference when Sam could prepare much of it in advance.

Sam noted that for Mr. Williams there had been an evening of visitation at Knight & Day the night before his funeral. As Jennifer had said, the funeral itself had taken place at First Episcopal Church, with Father Michael Hayes officiating. His funeral had been followed by a graveside committal ceremony at Collinsville Cemetery then a luncheon back at the church. These were all good signs that Carol Williams' children would be holding a full funeral for their mother as well.

After working steadily for some time and answering a few other phone calls and emails, Sam realized he was hungry. He stood to stretch his legs and made his way to the employee break room. In the hallway he passed Grace Gatekeeper, the company's junior-most funeral director. She was wearing earbuds, which she often did in odd moments throughout the day. She smiled sleepily and raised a palm to Sam. He noticed a smudge of toothpaste near the corner of her mouth.

"You've got some…," he mouthed and pointed to his own lips, gesturing for her to wipe the toothpaste away.

Grace sat down at her desk at Knight & Day Funeral Home after the transfer of Carol Williams, fired up Chrome, and Googled "Carol Williams Collinsville."

Up popped all kinds of mentions: gardening articles Carol had written for the community Master Gardener program; bowling tournament results; photos from a hospice fundraiser ten years ago; and a list of emeritus journalism professors from the local university.

The first inquiry Grace made for Carol Williams' funeral was to the best florist in town. "Dahlias," she told the floral shop manager with whom Grace often worked. "Can we get lots of dahlias?" Fortunately, dahlias were in season. The manager promised Grace that if the family wanted dahlias, she could source beautiful ones.

After hanging up with the florist, Grace popped in her earbuds and listened to one quick song while she caught up with texts from her roommate and friends. Then she returned to her notepad, where she'd written "bowling" in big letters.

She jumped up and hurried down to the office of John Knight, the funeral home's owner. Before making suggestions to Jennifer, Grace wanted to bounce a few ideas off him. In her four years at Knight & Day, she'd learned (the hard way in a couple of instances) that when it came to funeral service, the perceived line between creativity and crassness was sometimes a fine one.

Grace passed her older funeral director colleague, Sam Standard, in the hallway. Sam smiled and said good morning. Grace felt a rush of gratitude. She knew that Sam and the entire Knight & Day team were there to help her plan and carry out Carol Williams' funeral in the coming days.

After speaking with John Knight, the next call Grace made was to

Grace pulled the earbuds from her ears and rolled her eyes self-deprecatingly. "Thanks," she said. "I'm still half-asleep."

"I know the feeling," smiled Sam.

Back at his desk with a microwaved burrito and yet another cup of coffee, Sam phoned First Episcopal Church to inquire about their availability for a funeral later in the week. He spoke with the church secretary, who checked the church calendar and let him know the scheduling options. Sam knew that Reverend Hayes had retired some time ago but jotted down days and times that the current head rector, Reverend Zimmerman, would be available.

Sam also called the cemetery caretaker to tentatively schedule the committal ceremony. He then checked on Carol Williams in the Care Center, where the funeral home's embalmer, Ted, was just finishing up his work.

"She looks good," Sam told Ted. "I know it's hard after cancer. I'll call her daughter and let her know you're taking good care of her. Thank you."

Most of his initial preparations for Carol Williams' funeral now complete, Sam phoned Jennifer.

"I just checked on your mother," he immediately let her know. "Her body has been prepared. She looks good. Our Care Center staff has been taking good care of her."

"Oh, thank you," said Jennifer. "I keep finding myself thinking that she's still upstairs, but then I realize…"

"I understand," said Sam. "That's normal. When you come tomorrow, please bring whatever you would like her to wear in the casket. For women, we often recommend a dress or pantsuit,

Jennifer. "I was hoping you could tell me your mother's favorite color," Grace said.

"Pink," Jennifer said. "Definitely pink. Why?"

"I was just thinking…since she loved flowers, maybe she was a color person," Grace said. "Would it feel right to you to incorporate pink into the funeral? And dahlias? I just called the florist, and we're in luck. They're in season!"

"Dahlias and a pink funeral…," Jennifer mused. "It sounds perfect, actually. I mean, not fluorescent pink, but a rosy pink. Her favorite dress is that color. But…will pink be OK at the church?"

"That was another question I had for you," said Grace. "Did your mother attend a local church?"

"Well, she used to, back when my father was still alive," said Jennifer. "Dad's funeral was at First Episcopal. But to tell you the truth, Mom never seemed too connected to the church. She hasn't talked about it in a long time."

"What about you and your family?" asked Grace. "Do you belong to a church?"

"No," said Jennifer. "Does that mean we can't have a church funeral?"

"You can definitely have a church funeral if you want one," said Grace. "I'll call the Episcopal church and find out their availability. But tomorrow at the arrangement conference, I'll also share some other ideas about where the funeral could be held."

"Oh. OK," said Jennifer. "I never considered other places, but that might be nice."

"I Googled your mother," admitted Grace. "She led an amazing life. I look forward to helping you create a funeral as special as she was."

such as something they might have worn to church. But it's up to you. Anything you'd like."

"My mother was a pink person," laughed Jennifer. "I'll stop by her house and find something in her closet."

"I was able to find a lot of information in your father's file," continued Sam. "So I've filled out much of the paperwork already and have made initial calls to the Episcopal church and the cemetery. When you're here tomorrow, we'll put the finishing touches on the obituary and talk about anything else you and your family would like to make your mother's funeral just right."

Sam and Jennifer set a time for the arrangement conference the following day. Jennifer mentioned that her brother would also be attending. Sam then ran down the list of items Jennifer would want to bring with her. In addition to clothing for Carol, Jennifer should consider undergarments, socks or stockings, glasses, and jewelry. She should also bring a photo for the obituary and Carol's social security number for the death certificate.

"I've been on the phone all day, it seems," said Jennifer. "My head is spinning."

"Would you like me to text or email you a reminder list of the things to bring tomorrow?" asked Sam.

"I think that would be really helpful," sighed Jennifer. "Thank you. And thank you for being so kind. I don't know what I'm doing, but I feel like I'm in good hands."

"That's why I'm here," said Sam kindly. "To help you make decisions and make things as easy as possible. Please call me any time between now and our meeting tomorrow if you have any questions or if I can help in any way."

"The only thing she ever said about her own funeral was that she didn't want us to go to any trouble," said Jennifer. "'Just put me in a pine box and stick me in the garden,' she'd say."

"The most important thing I learned from my own mother's funeral as well as all the funerals I've helped plan at Knight & Day is that funerals may be *about* the person who died, but they're *for* the people still alive," said Grace gently. "The more special we make them, the more they properly honor a unique life—and the more they help those of us who grieve."

"I hadn't really thought about it before, but I'm starting to think you're right," said Jennifer. "I must warn you, though, that my brother, Jack, who'll also be coming to our meeting tomorrow, thinks we should skip all the fancy stuff and keep it simple."

"Don't worry," said Grace. "Everything is completely your choice. I'm here to help you and your brother understand the choices and also to educate you about why we often use certain elements of ceremony. From there it's up to you. Does your mother have a cemetery plot?" she added.

"Yes, next to my father at Collinsville Cemetery," said Jennifer.

"OK," said Grace. "I'll also notify the cemetery, and I'll get started on paperwork. We probably already have lots of the information we need from your father's funeral."

Grace and Jennifer set a time for the arrangement conference the next day. "Bring something for your mother to wear," said Grace. "Her favorite pink dress sounds perfect. Bring underwear and stockings, too. And you might want to dress her and do her hair and makeup yourself, but you can think about that. You won't have to do those things tomorrow."

After Sam hung up the phone, he immediately picked it up again to call his own elderly mother. He would stop by with take-out for her on his way home from work today, and he would spend at least an hour visiting and eating with her. One good thing about this job…on some days it served as a good reminder for you not to take the special people in your own life for granted.

After Grace hung up, she saw a reminder pop up on her phone screen. She'd almost forgotten about the fitting appointment she had for her bridesmaid dress over her lunch hour. Her best friend, Megan, was getting married in three weeks. Funerals and weddings. That seemed to be Grace's life lately—like that old movie *Three Weddings and a Funeral*, only for her, the ratio was closer to *Three Funerals and a Wedding*. Both are good, thought Grace. Both are meaningful, essential, and sacred.

1. First, what is your general impression of how Sam Standard handled the preparation? What about your general impression of Grace Gatekeeper's version?

2. Sam immediately turns to paperwork, while Grace immediately starts collecting more information about Carol Williams. What does this tell you about their different approaches? What might Grace have tried next if she hadn't been able to find out much about Carol Williams with a Google search?

3. From the beginning, Sam seems to assume that Carol Williams' family will want to make choices for her funeral that match the choices that were made for her husband's funeral. What do you think about this?

4. What clues can you find in this chapter and the previous chapter that Jennifer Jones and her family may not have wanted a church funeral? In what ways did Sam and Grace respond differently to those clues?

5. Sam and Grace handle differently the news that Carol Williams didn't want her family to go to any trouble after she died. What do you think about their two approaches?

6. In what unique ways do Sam and Grace prepare Jennifer Jones for the arrangement conference that will take place tomorrow?

CHAPTER 4

The Arrangement Conference, Part 1

In the Knight & Day Funeral Home lobby, Sam greeted Jennifer Jones and her brother, Jack Williams, with warm handshakes. He led them back to the arrangement room, where the three of them would be planning the funeral for Jennifer and Jack's mother, Carol Williams.

Sam carried three bottles of cold water to the table. "How is everyone doing?" he asked. His voice conveyed his genuine concern. "I'm sure it's been a hard couple of days."

Jennifer pressed her fingertips to her eyes. "Everyone's doing as well as can be expected," she sighed. "We've been phoning family and Mom's friends and neighbors. It's so exhausting, and I still feel like I'm in shock. But the casseroles are starting to pour in!" She chuckled.

Sam noticed that Jack had leaned back into his chair and crossed his arms over his chest. "Is this the first funeral you've been involved in planning, too, Jack?" Sam asked, attempting to engage him in the conversation.

"Yes," said Jack, his face a blank mask. "It's weird."

"I understand it can feel that way," said Sam. "But it's what I do every day. That's why I'm here: to help you and Jennifer make decisions and make things as easy as possible for you and your family.

"I'd like to start by filling you in on everything I've prepared so far," Sam began, opening his laptop in front of him. "Using information from your father's files, I was able to complete most of the paperwork already. I'll just need a few more details from you. I also called First Episcopal Church and have a list of the days and times that Reverend Zimmerman is available to officiate. And I've notified Collinsville Cemetery about the

In the Knight & Day Funeral Home lobby, Grace greeted Jennifer Jones and her brother, Jack Williams, with warm handshakes.

Grace led her guests to the arrangement room and helped them settle in. Focusing on hospitality, which the noted theologian Henri Nouwen described as "a sacred space where a stranger becomes a friend," she carried to the table a tasteful tray that held a glass pitcher of ice water, drinking glasses, a bowl of lemon slices, and individual packages of nuts, crackers, and dried fruit. She let them know where the restroom was, made sure the tissue box was in reach, and placed paper and pens on the table in case Jennifer and Jack wanted to jot anything down.

After a few initial moments of small talk, helping everyone feel more comfortable and dispel some of Jennifer and Jack's apparent and normal anxiety (Jack seemed particularly uncomfortable, crossing his arms over his chest and saying little), Grace thanked Jennifer for preparing the burial clothing for her mother, Carol Williams.

The day before, Grace had phoned Jennifer, offering to swing by Jennifer's house and pick up the clothing. This had allowed Knight & Day staff to have Carol dressed and prepared for Jennifer and Jack to visit privately during the arrangement conference—a practice Grace had begun offering more and more because she saw how much it helped families acknowledge the reality of the death and begin to embrace their normal and necessary pain.

Besides, throughout history people had always prepared and sat vigil with their dead loved ones themselves; Grace had grown to understand that the modern practice of separating dead bodies from their families often contributed to the discomfort with full funerals. The more she could help families understand that spending time with the body of their loved one was normal and natural, the more likely they were to open themselves to the healing possibilities of all the elements of funerals.

possibility of a committal service and opening the gravesite next to your father's."

"Oh, thank you," gushed Jennifer. "That sounds like a wonderful start. I can't tell you what a relief it is knowing that someone is taking care of everything. I can barely make it through the day, let alone plan…"

"Mom said she didn't want us to go to any trouble," Jack cut in. "All that sounds like a lot of trouble." He looked at his sister, who looked away.

Sam, prepared for Jack's objections, leaned toward Jack. "Tell us more about what you're thinking," Sam said respectfully.

"Well…" Jack recrossed his legs. "Just because we did all those things when Dad died doesn't mean we have to do them now. Mom wanted the full-meal deal for Dad, but she didn't want it for herself."

"What are we supposed to do then?" Jennifer asked. Her voice rose in anguish and frustration.

"I don't know," snapped Jack. "Maybe just cremation."

"Mom's money can pay for a funeral, if that's what you're worried about," Jennifer said. "And there are a lot of people who will want to pay respects, right? You made some phone calls to people this morning. You heard how much they cared about her."

"It's not just the money," said Jack. "It's all the rigmarole. She's dead, Jenn. Why throw a party for someone who's dead?"

Jennifer looked at Sam, her expression pleading for him to help her brother see reason. Negotiating family squabbles wasn't Sam's favorite part of the job, but unfortunately, it was a relatively common part.

"Your mother looks so nice in the pink dress you picked out for her," continued Grace. "No wonder it was her favorite color. After my own mother died and I became a funeral director, I realized that the bodies of those we love are still precious after they've died. And we only have a few days to spend with them before they leave us forever. Would you like to see your mom before we start talking about the funeral details?"

Jack looked away, but Jennifer held Grace's gaze. "Yes, I want to see her," she said finally, then she turned to her brother. "Jack, I know you're not sure about this, but I'd really like you to be with me. OK?"

After a moment's hesitation, Jack nodded a reluctant yes, and Grace led them to the intimate visitation room, where a simple white pillar candle cast a soft glow. Jennifer approached her mother. She put her hand to her mouth, and her eyes went wide. She held onto Jack's arm with one hand and reached out to touch her mother's arm with the other. There were no words as the two siblings took in the reality that their precious mother was really dead.

Grace backed away, recognizing that the brother and sister needed some private time with the body that had animated the life of their mother. When she quietly returned to the room ten minutes later, she saw that Jack, silent and stoic before, had now wrapped his arms around his sister and was holding her as they spoke softly to one another.

Soon Jennifer let Grace know that she and Jack were ready to go back to the arrangement room. There, Grace poured them water. She could see that Jennifer and Jack were working on moving from understanding their mother's death with their heads to understanding it with their hearts. In mortuary school, Grace had learned that honoring exploration leads to understanding leads to taking action. So she knew that before diving into funeral planning, Jennifer and Jack

"Jennifer, I hear you saying that your mother has other family and friends who will want to come to the funeral and pay their respects," Sam said, employing his active listening and paraphrasing skills. "Jack, I hear you saying that your mother didn't want you to go to any trouble. You're also not comfortable with the idea of a full funeral, is that right?"

"That about sums it up," Jack said. He uncrossed his arms and reached for his bottled water. "Besides, you said you were going to make this as easy as possible for us."

"I did say that," Sam confirmed. "And I meant it. I think we can find ways to plan a simple funeral that works for both of you. How does that sound?"

"That sounds good to me," said Jennifer.

"Me too," said Jack.

"All right," said Sam. "Let's talk about some of your options…"

first needed to process the profound experience they'd just shared. Reminding herself to go slowly and follow the family's lead, she allowed for a few minutes of sacred silence.

"She already looks so much better than she did when you took her yesterday," Jennifer finally said. "The cancer really ravaged her. Her hair isn't quite right, though."

"If you'd like," Grace offered, "you can adjust her hair and makeup yourself the day before the visitation. It's a nice way to be involved and spend time with the body."

"I'll think about that," said Jennifer.

"I don't know what I was expecting," said Jack, "but it wasn't as bad as I thought it would be. It's not Mom, but it's still Mom, you know? And she's still right here, in this building."

Grace allowed Jennifer and Jack to continue sharing thoughts about their mother's body, offering her own comments only occasionally to affirm that their reactions were understandable and normal.

Soon, though, the conversation segued naturally to Carol Williams' life. Grace remarked that she'd learned a lot about Carol online. "She was involved in this community for a long time, wasn't she?" asked Grace. "I know you mentioned some of these things at your house, but she was a Master Gardener, a bowler, and a hospice volunteer. And she taught journalism at the university!"

Over the next ten minutes, Jennifer and Jack told Grace stories about their childhoods and their mother's vibrant life then her decline into cancer and death. The siblings both cried and laughed as they reflected on memories.

"OK," Jack finally said, giving his hands a clap. "What's next?"

"Now we talk about creating a funeral as special as your mother was," said Grace.

"But Mom wanted something simple," said Jack. "She told us a bunch of times that she didn't want us to go to any trouble."

"That's so common for dying people to say—especially mothers," said Grace. "My own said the same thing. But what I learned was that funerals are actually for those of us left behind to grieve. So I want you two to make whatever choices are best for you and the rest of your family and friends. But as we talk, would it be OK if I shared a little about why we do each of the things we often do as part of a meaningful funeral? Then you'll be prepared to make informed choices."

"That sounds good to me," said Jennifer.

"Me too," said Jack.

"Good," said Grace. "Let's get started."

QUESTIONS FOR REFLECTION:

1. What little differences in hospitality do you note between Sam and Grace? Explain whether or not you think the small touches create a different impression or set a different tone.

2. How does Jennifer and Jack's private time with their mother's body (or lack thereof, on Sam's side) affect the beginning of the arrangement conference?

3. Jack is a funeral skeptic. In your opinion, what are the main reasons he seems opposed to having a full funeral for his mother? How do Sam's and Grace's early interactions with him differ, and how do those differences establish the boundaries of what will and won't be possible for Carol Williams' funeral? What experiences do you have with reluctant or downright hostile family members?

4. Grace takes a few moments to explicitly teach Jennifer and Jack about the importance of spending time with the body. Later in the conversation, she asks their permission to continue to teach them about why the different elements of the funeral are often used. What do you think about Grace's educational approach?

5. Grace seems to have a gift for pacing her interactions with at-need families to build trust and give them time to mourn. What can we learn from her?

6. You've probably noticed that Grace is spending a bit more time with Jennifer and Jack than Sam is. How long would you estimate Sam's arrangement conference has taken so far? What about Grace's? What do you think about the time difference?

CHAPTER 5

The Arrangement Conference, Part 2

"OK, first let's talk about whether or not you want to have a visitation for your mother," Sam said to Jennifer and Jack. "That decision may help us make some of the other decisions more efficiently."

"That's the part where people come hang out with the dead body?" Jack asked, folding his arms over his chest.

Jennifer's sigh was pained.

"Yes, the body is generally in a casket in the room during the visitation," Sam said. "The casket can be closed, however, if you'd prefer."

"We had a visitation for Dad," Jennifer said. "Do you remember how many people came? So many!"

"What I remember is standing in a line and shaking the hands of a million people I didn't know," Jack said. "It was exhausting. Plus, Dad was younger when he died, and more of his friends were still around to show up for the visitation. I think it's mainly a tradition for older people. And having Dad's dead body in a casket in the corner was just…bizarre."

Jennifer looked unsure of what to think or say next. She turned to Sam for help.

"The visitation is definitely optional," Sam said. "It's also possible to have a short viewing period at the church on the morning of the funeral, right before the service."

"That might be good," Jennifer said. "How about that, Jack?"

"Mom was so sick that she didn't look like herself anymore," Jack said more softly now, reaching over to touch his sister's arm. "I think everyone would rather remember her how she was, before the cancer. You know?"

"In the same way that it was moving for you to visit your mother's body just now, it is also moving and helpful for others who cared about her to spend time with the body," Grace said to Jennifer and Jack. "It's hard for our minds and hearts to really understand that someone is no longer alive, so seeing and touching the body helps us make this necessary transition. That's why funerals often include a day—or sometimes more than one day—of public visitation."

"I want to have a visitation for Mom," Jennifer said, taking both of Jack's hands in hers and looking him in the eye. "So many people loved her, including our kids, Jack. They need to be able to say good-bye."

"But won't it be hard for them to see her…dead?" Jack asked. "It's hard for me."

"I hope it is OK for me to explain that any child old enough to love is old enough to mourn," Grace said. "I can help you support them through this important time as you teach them that death is a natural part of life. They will always remember that you helped them be a part of the funeral."

"All right," Jack said. "But how much of this visitation do we need?"

"Well, lots of people knew and loved Mom," Jennifer said. "Can we have at least an afternoon and an evening—and maybe even some time before the service?"

"Jennifer, we can do whatever best meets your needs and the needs of your family and friends," Grace said. "By having ample time for visitation, you are essentially inviting the community to participate in mourning your mother and supporting your family. We have found that when families forego visitation, people often take that as a sign that the family doesn't want support. It's like the door for communication and empathy never gets opened. You should be proud of yourselves for

"Maybe you're right," said Jennifer.

"All right," Sam said equably. "No public visitation. Let's talk about the ceremony. As I mentioned earlier, I already called First Episcopal Church and have a list of the days and times that Reverend Zimmerman is available to officiate." He found his notes and showed them to Jennifer and Jack. "Which of these do you think might work best for your family?"

Jennifer and Jack scanned the list of dates and times.

"I guess it might be easier for everyone to make it on Saturday morning," Jennifer said. "My older son works but has weekends off."

"I agree," Jack said. "My daughter, Claire, is in college a few hours away, but she could be here on Saturday."

"All right, I'll call the church as soon as we're done meeting to reserve that time," said Sam. "You'll be planning the ceremony itself with Reverend Zimmerman. Here's the phone number you'll need to schedule a meeting with him."

"Another meeting?" groaned Jack.

"Reverend Zimmerman will help you with music selections, readings, the eulogy, and other details of the service," said Sam. "He's a very nice man and an experienced minister. I'm sure you'll like him."

"Jack, I can handle that meeting if you want," said Jennifer. "Clark will come with me."

"OK. Maybe. Thanks," Jack said.

"So next, the service at the church is often followed by a brief committal ceremony at the cemetery," Sam explained. "I believe you had one of those for your father?"

inviting people to come mourn with and support you.

"And the visitation can be made even more meaningful if it's personalized with special touches," Grace added. "The florist told me we can get dahlias, which could be placed around the room. Maybe the grandchildren would want to help by putting together a photo display and picking out music your mother loved? Our sound system can play it softly in the background."

"Dahlias! That would be so nice!" Jennifer said through tears. "And we'll talk to the grandkids about how they might like to be involved."

"OK," Grace said. "One more suggestion for making the visitation meaningful is to invite guests to sign not only their names to the registration book but also jot down a memory of how your mother touched their lives. I can help you set that up if you'd like."

"That sounds nice," Jennifer said.

"Great. We can firm up details later," Grace said. "Now for the funeral ceremony, Jennifer and I talked about the possibility of holding it at First Episcopal church, where your father's was. I've looked into the openings they have. I also wanted you to know that if you'd rather, the funeral ceremony could be held somewhere else. Would you like to hear a couple of ideas?"

"Sure," Jack said. "Mom wasn't a big church person. We're not either."

"I called the university, and since your mother is an emeritus professor there, her funeral could be held in their chapel, on the campus," Grace said. "It's a lovely little church, but it's still a church."

"Oh!" Jennifer said, leaning in and smiling. "I've never been there!

"Besides the two church options, I had one more idea," said Grace. "Collinsville Community Gardens. They are also available for a private

"Yes, we did," Jennifer said.

"Oh yeah," Jack said. "It rained. I don't get why people have a ceremony at the church and then another ceremony at the cemetery. Isn't that overkill?"

"Well, one ceremony is more about remembering the life, and one is about laying the body to rest," said Sam.

"The only thing Mom ever told us is that she didn't want us to go to too much trouble after she died," Jack said emphatically. "I think she'd be more than happy with the church service and leave it at that."

"Can we have a funeral without the cemetery part?" asked Jennifer. "What happens to the casket?"

"If you'd rather, the minister may be able to include the committal prayers in the service held at the church," said Sam. "After the church service, our staff would take the casket to the cemetery, and the cemetery staff would handle the burial. You could visit your mother's grave the next day, after the casket is already in the ground."

"Oh," said Jennifer. She looked down. The worry lines in her forehead seemed deeply etched.

"What do you think, Sis?" Jack asked gently.

"I think I'm going to miss her so much," Jennifer sobbed.

"Me too," Jack whispered, and he moved to wrap his sister in a tight hug.

Sam slid the tissue box on the table closer to the siblings.

"I tell you what," Sam said. "Let's take a brief break. The two of you can talk privately about whether or not to have a committal service, and I'll go check on a few things. You might also want service on Saturday morning. They have a building that would fit about a hundred people, and they have an outdoor pavilion that would hold even more. We could add a white event tent if we needed more space."

"Mom would love the idea of a funeral in a flower garden," Jennifer said. "And everything's in bloom right now. It would be so beautiful!"

"Yes," Grace said. "I've found that any place can be sacred if it honors the person who died and holds the community of people who are joined by their love and memories of that person."

"Her garden was her favorite place," Jack agreed. He looked at his sister. "I appreciate the university chapel and Episcopal church ideas, but I think the community garden seems right—though I've never been to a funeral anywhere like that."

"We can have the funeral wherever you feel best meets the needs of your family," Grace said. "Today's families are realizing that they find meaning in a location that speaks to them and the person who died.

"Of course, the committal service at Collinsville Cemetery will also be outdoors," Grace added. "I stopped by your mother and father's spaces yesterday and took these photos." She showed Jennifer and Jack some shots on her phone. "Everything's green and lush, and the snowball bushes near the headstone are blooming like crazy. So pretty."

"The committal service…that's the part where you have another ceremony right after the ceremony you just attended?" Jack asked. "I don't get that."

"The committal service is where you and your family and friends accompany your mother to her final resting place," Grace said. "It's where the final good-byes are said to the precious body that all of you loved so very much. The committal helps our brains acknowledge the reality of the death. It also helps our hearts know that we didn't to use the restrooms, which are right around the corner." He pointed. "Then when I come back, we'll finish up with the last details, including the gathering after the funeral, the obituary, and casket selection."

"Perfect," Jack said. "Thank you for your help. We've never done this before, and it's not easy."

"I'm glad I can make it easier for you," Sam said.

Sam left the arrangement room and closed the door softly behind him. He headed to the office of his uncle and the funeral home's owner, John Knight, for a quick hello and update.

It felt good to stretch his legs and clear his own head. He sighed, remembering that his children were visiting this weekend and that now he would likely be tied up with Carol Williams' funeral.

But such was the life of a funeral director. He really was glad that he could help make this difficult time as simple and smooth as possible for Jennifer, Jack, and their families.

leave the body to be buried alone, by strangers. Instead, we cherished, safeguarded, and paid respects to the body right to the very end."

"I see," Jennifer said. "It's like Jack and I are the caretakers of her body now—with Knight & Day's help. And our caretaking responsibility isn't over until she's buried."

"Yes," Grace said. "It is a sacred responsibility. And we wrap ritual around all of that—music, readings, prayers, etcetera—because only ritual is powerful enough to express our profound thoughts and feelings. Everyday words and actions just aren't enough."

"OK," Jack said. "I get that now. The committal is like the conclusion of the funeral ceremony. Without it, there's no ending."

"Exactly," Grace said. "Now let's take a short break, then we'll talk more about this special funeral for your very special mother."

1. From the opening paragraph, Sam and Grace approach the topic of the visitation differently with Jennifer and Jack. What can we learn from each of their styles?

2. In general, what has been your experience talking to families about visitation? If you are a funeral director in training, have you been present yet at any arrangement conferences? If so, how was the visitation discussion handled?

3. How do Sam and Grace handle the subject of the committal ceremony differently? What can we learn from each of their approaches?

4. Notice that both Sam and Grace are educating along the way. Sam, however, tends to educate about procedures, and Grace chooses to educate about the reasons behind the processes and funeral elements. What is the effect of each approach on Jennifer and Jack?

5. Sam's focus on simple and efficient creates a different arrangement conference atmosphere. Which adjectives would you use to describe that atmosphere? Which would you use to describe the atmosphere of Grace's arrangement conference?

CHAPTER 6

The Arrangement Conference, Part 3

Sam brought Jennifer and Jack more water and sat down across the arrangement table from them once again.

"We'll submit the obituary electronically to the newspaper for you," Sam said. "I was able to pull a draft together by referring to your father's obituary. Please look this over and see what might be missing or incorrect."

Sam slid Jennifer and Jack a printout of Carol Williams' draft obituary.

"Looks pretty standard," Jack nodded.

"What about her career? Shouldn't that be included?" asked Jennifer. "She was a journalism professor at Colorado University for a long time."

"Oh, certainly," said Sam, jotting down notes. "Did you bring a photo you would like to use?"

"I think the last formal portrait she had taken was for the church directory," Jennifer said. "But that was years ago... Would they still have it?"

"After our meeting, I'll call First Episcopal and see if I can get that photo," Sam said. "Speaking of the church, will you be having a reception or luncheon there after the ceremony?"

"That's what you do, right?" said Jack. "Egg-salad sandwiches and bad coffee?"

Sam smiled. "Well, usually the church has a committee of women who prepare food for and host the reception," he said. "They're very nice and very helpful."

"I guess that would be fine," said Jennifer. "So we should talk to the minister about it when we meet with him to plan the ceremony?"

"When I contact First Episcopal to confirm the service and ask

"All right," Grace said when she and Jennifer and Jack were back seated at the arrangement conference table. "We've decided to have a visitation, a funeral ceremony at the Collinsville Community Gardens, and a brief committal service at the cemetery. Now let's talk about some of the elements of the funeral ceremony. First, are you interested in a religious service led by a clergyperson, or would you rather have a more secular service?"

"Mom was raised in the Methodist church and attended the Episcopal church with Dad for a long time," Jennifer said. "But she wasn't really religious. And as we've said, we're not, either."

"I've worked with a funeral celebrant named Sophie Blue a number of times," said Grace. "She helps families like yours put together a ceremony that is meaningful to you without being overtly religious. Is that something you'd be interested in?"

"That sounds perfect," Jennifer said.

"OK, let me send her a quick text to see if she's available." Grace pecked at her phone for a moment then turned her attention back to Jennifer and Jack.

"Sophie will help you pick out readings and music and also figure out ways for the people who loved your mother most to be part of the ceremony," Grace said, "like doing readings, playing music, and being pallbearers. She'll lead the service, kind of like an emcee. She'll also help you capture your mother's life and your love for her, maybe with a photo slide show or video and a personalized eulogy."

"We need to remember that Mom didn't want us to go to too much trouble," reminded Jack. "Let's not go overboard."

"Telling the story of your mom's life is for your family and for all the people who cared about her," Grace said gently. "It's how you express your love. It's not really for your mom—although maybe you wonder, about the photo, I'll let them know you'd like the reception there, too," Sam said. "That way it will get on the committee's calendar as soon as possible."

"There's so much to do!" sighed Jennifer. "It's like planning a wedding or a graduation party—but in just a few days."

"You're right—there's a lot to do and not a lot of time to do it," Sam said. "But just remember that I'm here to help however I can. Plus, you'll find the church folks have processes and systems in place that carry a lot of the burden. They've done this many, many times.

"Now, do you have certain people in mind to be pallbearers?" asked Sam. "They'll carry the casket from the hearse into the church then, after the service, from the church back to the hearse. Caskets are heavy, so six men usually works well."

Jennifer and Jack spent a few minutes coming up with a list of people they would ask to be pallbearers, including their own children.

"It's sad that they have to think about death when they're so young and full of life themselves," said Jennifer. "I think this funeral is going to be hard for them. They were little when their granddad died, but this they'll never be able to forget."

Jack squeezed his sister's arm. "They're resilient," he said. "They'll be OK."

"All right, just a couple of things left," said Sam. "Let's look at casket options." He pulled up the casket selection website on his laptop and walked around the table so he could sit beside Jennifer and Jack. "I'm thinking you might be interested in a casket similar to the one your father was buried in? It's common for couples to have matching or complementary caskets."

as I do, if she gets to 'watch' the funeral too. Besides, I've found that it takes about the same amount of effort to put together a generic ceremony as it does a personalized ceremony."

"OK," Jack said, though he still didn't look totally convinced. "You're the expert here."

"No, *you're* the expert," Grace said. "My role is to help you understand the possibilities and the reasons why certain choices can be helpful. Your role is to choose what's best for you and your family." She glanced back at her phone. "Sophie texted back," she said. "She's available to work on your mom's funeral. Do you think that's the way you want to go?"

Jennifer and Jack looked at each other for confirmation. Jennifer spoke. "Yes, we'll use Sophie as celebrant. The amazing thing is, now that we've gotten this far in the planning process, I'm actually getting excited about Mom's funeral. I mean, I'm still really devastated"—she choked back a sob—"but I'm also realizing that with your help and with Sophie's help we can put together a simple but beautiful ceremony that we'll remember forever."

"I agree," Grace said. "And I think you're really going to like Sophie. I'll arrange a meeting for you with her here at Knight & Day tomorrow. I'll be in that meeting, too. Now, let's talk about the obituary. I've taken the liberty of drafting one up, using details I was able to pull from your father's obituary as well as information about your mom I found online. Please read over this draft and let's fill in any gaps."

She slid a printed page over to Jennifer and Jack, who bowed their heads together to read.

"Oh, I like how you put that in there about her being a gardener and a bowler," said Jennifer. "And her career at the university. I think those are the highlights!"

"Did you bring a photo of her for the obituary?" asked Grace.

Sam pulled up an image of a gleaming wooden model. "Your father was buried in this casket," he said. "It's made of walnut. The interior lining was off-white, which is standard, but you can also choose a special lining color for your mother, if you'd like."

"It looks so big," Jennifer said. "The cancer had made Mom so tiny at the end."

"It looks expensive," Jack said.

"Mom's money will pay for it," Jennifer said. "Let's not get hung up on cost."

"Caskets are a pretty standard size," Sam said. "Maybe you'd like something more feminine for your mom?"

"If we're not going to worry about cost, then I think we should get the casket that matches Dad's," Jack said. "That makes the decision simple."

"All right," Jennifer sighed. "That's fine."

Sam helped Jennifer and Jack select a guest book and thank-you note cards, then the conversation turned to flowers.

"Usually there's a casket spray from the family," Sam said. "That's the main arrangement that's placed on top of the casket."

"Oh, Mom just loved flowers," said Jennifer, wiping her eyes with a tissue. "She was a gardener, you know."

"Here are some photos of casket sprays our florist has put together in the past," Sam said, flipping through a small book. "Which of these looks nice to you?"

Jennifer took the book in her hands and turned the pages. "This is pretty," she said as she pointed to a large arrangement of pinks and purples. "This looks like Mom."

"Yes, you encouraged me to choose a picture that I loved," said Jennifer, "so I pulled this one from a frame in my house. It's my favorite."

Grace held the photo. In it, Carol Williams wore a floppy gardening hat and an ear-to-ear smile. "What a special photo," Grace said. "We can use it not only for the obituary but also for the memorial folders, guest book cover, and signage, if you'd like. I'll submit the obituary and photo to the newspaper and get them on Knight & Day's website right away, too. So many people today look for obituaries and sign virtual guest books online, then share them via social media. It's a wonderful way to pass along news of your mother's death and also invite as many people as possible to her visitation and funeral. Now, have you given any thought to the reception after the committal service?"

"Do we have to feed people?" Jack groaned.

"Well, if my experience after the death of my mother is any indication, people will be feeding you," laughed Grace. "They'll be bringing you cakes and casseroles for weeks. But yes, on the day of the funeral, the family usually hosts a gathering. It's not just about food, though. It's about community and sharing memories. It's about people supporting each other and making plans together for the future. Did you have a church luncheon after your father's funeral?"

"Yes," Jack said. "Egg-salad sandwiches and bad coffee."

"I'll give you a list of local restaurants and cafés that cater events like this," Grace said. "You could have the gathering in your home. Or the caterer could set up an area in the Community Gardens building with simple refreshments—maybe just finger food and lemonade, but that's totally up to you."

"All right. We'll call around," Jennifer said.

Next, Grace helped Jack and Jennifer select a large guest book—one that had room for people to write down a special memory in addition

"What about all the flowers people send, though?" asked Jack. "What are we supposed to do with all of them?"

"In the obituary, we could suggest that in lieu of flowers, a donation be made to a cause your mother cared about," Sam said.

"How about the Collinsville Community Gardens?" Jennifer asked.

"Sounds good," Jack said.

"All right," Sam said. "I think we've covered everything. Here's a folder with paperwork noting the decisions we've made today. Take this with you. Don't forget to set up a meeting with Reverend Zimmerman. Here's his number. I'll let you know if I can't get your mother's photo from the church. And I'll be phoning you over the next few days when other details come up."

"Thanks," Jack said, shaking Sam's hand. "You've been a big help."

"I'm glad I can make things easier for you," Sam said as he walked the brother and sister to the door. "Call me if you have any questions at any time, day or night, OK?"

to their names—and thank-you note cards.

"Before you go, we also need to pick out a casket," Grace said. "Is there a certain type or look you had in mind?"

"Dad's was elaborate," Jennifer said, "all dark wood and satin. I can't see a casket like that in a flower garden."

"Do you have something more simple?" Jack asked. "Like the proverbial pine box?"

"Actually, there are lovely pine caskets," Grace said. "And because we're honoring your mother's love of gardening, you might want to add a gardening-themed cap panel. Would you like to look at some options?"

Jennifer and Jack nodded, and Grace pulled up casket images on her laptop, turning the screen so everyone could see. Jennifer and Jack chose a simple, light pine casket and a floral cap panel.

"Now, we've already decided to have lots of dahlias, right?" asked Grace. "Would you like a spray of dahlias for the top of the casket from your family?"

"Definitely," said Jennifer. "The more dahlias, the better."

"All right," Grace said, smiling at her guests. "I think we've covered everything we need to for today. Here's a folder with paperwork. I'll text both of you the time for the meeting with Sophie."

Grace stood to walk Jennifer and Jack out of Knight & Day. When they reached the siblings' car, Grace gave each of them a quick hug. "You did great work today," she said. "Your mom's funeral is going to be wonderful. I'll see you tomorrow. In the meantime, call or text me if you have any more questions or ideas. Just like with the dahlias, the more ideas, the better. "

QUESTIONS FOR REFLECTION:

1. Notice how Grace asks the family if they would like a religious ceremony, where in both this and the last chapter, Sam assumes it. How do you imagine at this point that the funerals will play out differently as a result of their unique approaches?

2. Grace suggests to Jennifer and Jack that they can use an independent funeral celebrant to plan and lead the service. What do you think of this idea and why?

3. In what ways do Sam and Grace handle the obituary and the photo of Carol Williams differently? What are the different results?

4. In this chapter, Grace says that it takes about the same amount of effort to put together a generic ceremony as a personalized ceremony. Do you agree or disagree? Why?

5. At a funeral, flower arrangements are a tangible display of people's love and support. How does Sam and Grace's guidance about this differ, and what might be the net result?

6. Sam and Grace approach casket selection somewhat similarly, yet their guidance leads the family in two different directions. What are the subtle cues they give that result in divergent choices?

CHAPTER 7

The Arrangement Conference, Part 4

GRACE GATEKEEPER

(Note: Under Sam Standard's direction, the funeral ceremony planning itself is now in the hands of Reverend Zimmerman at First Episcopal Church and so will not be covered here.)

The day after the arrangement conference, Grace hosted the meeting between the funeral celebrant, Sophie Blue, and siblings Jennifer Jones and Jack Williams, with her usual focus on hospitality and attention to detail.

After introducing everyone and making sure simple refreshments were close at hand, Grace asked Jennifer and Jack if it was OK with them if she set the stage for the meeting with a brief review of the purposes of funerals. They nodded in agreement, and Grace slid a brochure featuring a multi-colored triangle onto the table.

Transcendence

Meaning

Expression

Support

Recall

Reality

"This simple graphic shows the important reasons why we have had funerals since the beginning of time," Grace said.

"Yes, I noticed you also have a poster of that graphic hanging on your wall," said Jack.

"We do," said Grace. "It serves as a reminder of why the four of us are gathered here today. First, funerals help us acknowledge the **reality** that someone precious has died." As she mentioned each layer of the pyramid, Grace pointed at it. "They give us a time and place to do the work of remembering and sharing those memories, which is what **recall** means. Of course, funerals are also social experiences, which means they bring people together to **support** one another. **Expression** means that in order to begin to heal, we need to share our grief thoughts and feelings outside of ourselves. The funeral is an essential time for mourning, and as you express your feelings, that is what you're doing. **Meaning** and **transcendence** are more spiritual tasks we begin to work on at the funeral. We listen to stories and consider the meaning of the life of the person who died—and the meaning of life in general. And finally, funerals help wake us up to what's really important and precious in our lives, putting us on a path toward eventually transcending our grief and living and loving even more fully. What's more, the other purposes of the funeral—reality, recall, support, expression, and meaning—form a bridge that takes us back to our community and to our changed lives. The bridge is how we begin to transcend the death."

"Huh," Jack said. "I never thought about funerals like that. I don't have a lot of experience with them, but to me they always seemed more like a bother or an unnecessary obligation—especially since the guest of honor is dead."

"This funeral is, of course, about honoring and remembering your mother, but you and your families and friends are actually the guests of honor," Grace said gently. "A good funeral will help all of you acknowledge your grief, allow yourself to mourn, wrestle with the meaning of everything, and receive support from others. It helps everyone know what to do when mere words are inadequate. But in my work as a funeral director, I've seen too many funerals that confuse efficiency with effectiveness. Families and even sometimes those of us in funeral service tend to think that the best funeral is easy and painless. As a result, they end up skipping many of the healing pieces of funerals and creating cookie-cutter ceremonies that don't fulfill the purposes of the funeral we've reviewed together. The family and friends return home feeling empty. It's a shame, because it's such a wasted opportunity. Funerals are about a good beginning on the path to healing. Sophie and I are going to do the best we can to make sure you and your family and friends get off to a good start."

"I've been to a couple of generic funerals," nodded Jennifer. "They didn't seem to be about the person who died or the family. They *did* feel like an unnecessary obligation, Jack—like sending a Christmas card with no personal note or even a photo, just a signature."

Sophie spoke up. "OK!" she said. "It sounds like we're all in agreement about planning a meaningful funeral. Here's another image that's helpful for us to keep in mind as we plan. This heart depicts most of the pieces of the funeral that we'll be talking about during this meeting. When they're combined, they create a whole that is more meaningful than the sum of the individual parts."

What followed was an animated discussion about all the pieces that would come together for Carol Williams' funeral. What music did she love? What music would resonate with the family? Could

Music

Readings

Visitation/Reception

Eulogy/Remembrance

Symbols

Gathering

Actions

anyone they knew play the piano or another instrument or sing? Which spiritual texts or poems sprang to mind? How would the eulogy be structured? Could multiple people share memories and speak about different parts of Carol's multidimensional life? Who could pull together photos for a tribute video of Carol's life? What symbols—besides Carol's beloved dahlias, which they'd already agreed would be present in profusion—did the family find meaningful—the Christian cross, candles, water, stones, angels, incense? What actions could friends and family members take—sometimes individually, sometimes together—as a way of participating in and enriching the ceremony?

As Sophie facilitated the conversation and Jennifer, Jack, and Grace contributed ideas and "ahas!", Sophie's notepad filled with choices that sometimes made Jennifer and even Jack smile with excitement over the richness of the ceremony they now understood was being created, and sometimes brought them to tears as they felt the pain of the loss and explored their mother's life.

Soon Sophie was making to-do lists for each of them to work on—people to ask to participate in the ceremony in various ways, photos and memorabilia to gather, details to be nailed down about the food at the reception.

Finally, Jennifer sat back in her chair and breathed a big sigh. "I feel really drained," she said, rubbing her eyes. "But in a good way. This is going to a really good funeral, isn't it?"

"I think you're right, Jenn," said Jack. "And I'm learning it's really not that complicated. But we wouldn't have known what to do or why to do it if it wasn't for your help, Grace and Sophie."

"Between now and Saturday, Sophie and I are here to help you dot all the Is and cross all the Ts," Grace said. "We'll stay in contact about all the details. Let us know if you run into any obstacles or need help of any kind with anything. That's what we do. That's why we're here."

Grace reached out her hands across the table, taking one of Jennifer's hands and one of Jack's. She squeezed. "Your mother was so lucky to have you both in her life," she said softly. "Your love for her has lit up this room today."

After the tissue box was passed, the four people went their separate ways, tired but also energized by the meaningful funeral experience they knew in their hearts they had been privileged to help plan that day.

QUESTIONS FOR REFLECTION:

1. Some funeral homes have celebrants on staff; some call on the services of independent celebrants, as you see in this book. Other funeral homes have not chosen to work with celebrants but instead rely on local clergy to officiate services. This chapter depicts the role and possibilities of a non-church-affiliated celebrant. How does involving Sophie in the funeral planning affect the coming service?

2. In this meeting, Grace and Sophie explain both the reasons why we have funerals and the common elements of funerals. Do you think this kind of education is helpful to and/or necessary for at-need families? Why or why not?

3. While Sam is not involved in the church funeral planning, Grace participates in the planning session with the funeral celebrant. How do you feel about funeral directors being involved in such detailed service planning?

4. This meeting is, in effect, a second arrangement conference for Grace with Carol Williams' family. What do you think about that?

5. Grace's relationship with Jennifer and Jack continues to grow closer as she works with them to plan a unique and individualized service for their mother. How do you establish appropriate boundaries between funeral directors and the families they serve?

CHAPTER 8

The Visitation

GRACE GATEKEEPER

(Note: Under Sam Standard's direction, the decision was made to have no public visitation for Carol Williams and so will not be covered here.)

Before Jennifer and Jack arrived, along with their families, to host their mother's visitation, Grace Gatekeeper spent a few minutes in the visitation room making sure everything was ready.

The centerpiece of the pink table-clothed greeting table was a large framed photo of Carol Williams—the same lovely gardening snapshot that anchored the detailed and loving obituary that ran the last two days in the local newspaper and had been accessed online by community members many times that week. Keepsake copies of the obituary, tastefully designed and printed on nice stationery paper, sat in a stack next to the oversized guest book. In addition to signing their names, friends and family members would be invited to jot down a brief memory or thought about Carol.

Displayed on another table were special items that helped tell the story of Carol's life—more photos, a couple textbooks from her journalism professor days, her favorite bowling ball, her gardening trowel and hat, the most special of the angel figurines she collected, and of course, a simple vase of her favorite flowers—pink dahlias.

Grace clicked on the sound system, and the violins' sweet tones from one of Carol's favorite tunes—Louis Armstrong's "What a Wonderful World"—began to glide through the air. The family had provided a playlist of music that would loop in the background throughout the visitation that afternoon and then again, after a dinner and rest break for the family, later that evening. Grace adjusted the volume so the music wouldn't be obtrusive, then she dimmed the room's lighting slightly and walked to the casket, which was surrounded by more than a dozen floral arrangements that had been sent by distant family and friends as well as local friends.

Carol Williams lay in her favorite pink dress in a simple light-pine casket. As Jennifer and Jack had noted during their private time with their mother a couple of days ago, Carol looked restful, even restored, after her harrowing battle with pancreatic cancer. Jennifer had even come that morning to do Carol's hair and makeup herself. The casket's embroidered cap panel—an airy spray of pink roses—provided a lovely and personalized finishing touch.

Grace heard footsteps behind her and turned to see John Knight, the funeral home's owner, enter the visitation room.

"It looks like you've done an exceptional job in here, as usual," he said. "Is there anything I can do to help?"

"No, thanks," Grace said. "I think Sophie and I have everything covered." Sophie Blue was the funeral celebrant who had helped plan the ceremony and would be leading the funeral and committal tomorrow.

"I understand the ceremony is going to be held at Collinsville Community Gardens," John Knight said. "That's the first time we've done that. I think it's a great idea."

Grace shrugged as if it was the most obvious choice in the world. "Our Carol here loved gardens and flowers. It's where she should be when all the people who loved her gather to celebrate her life and mourn her death."

Grace and John Knight left the visitation room, and soon it was time for Grace to meet Jennifer and Jack and their families at Knight & Day's front door. She gave Jennifer and Jack a hug—engaged funeral planning tends to make people rather intimate friends quickly—then gently said hello and introduced herself to their spouses and children.

When it was time to lead the families into the visitation room, Grace walked slowly, with Jennifer and Jack at her side. She could feel the natural tension in the group, and with her measured movements, wanted to affirm to everyone that this "moment of truth" was indeed difficult but also normal and necessary.

Grace also knew that because Jennifer and Jack had already had private viewing time with their mother, and because Jennifer had done Carol's hair and makeup, the siblings were now comfortable with the idea of spending time with the precious body that had animated the life of their mother. They, in turn, would help make their spouses and children comfortable, which would then help put all the visitation guests at ease as they arrived throughout the day to pay their respects.

Grace opened the door and motioned for Jennifer and Jack to step inside first. After everyone had entered the visitation room, Grace herself walked in and closed the door quietly behind her. She stood at the back of the room, unobtrusive yet present, as some family members approached the casket while others hung back. After a few minutes of tears and hugs and whispers, Grace watched as one by one the family members grew comfortable. Their body language began to relax, and they slowly transitioned to speaking more normally, at regular conversational volumes. They were learning how to be with their beloved mother and grandmother even in death—and with each other at this heartbreaking time. And they were learning that death is as normal and natural as life.

Soon Jennifer and Jack walked over to Grace. "Oh, this song!" Jennifer gasped and put her right palm to her heart. "And look at all the flowers!"

"Yes, many people sent arrangements," Grace said. "Your mother and your family are clearly well loved."

"I always thought funeral flowers were kind of a waste," Jack said, walking over to read the gift cards on each arrangement. "Nobody wants to take this many flowers home, and they just die…but standing here right now I can see that it's not about the flowers, really. It's a way for all these people to let us know they care and that they're here with us right now in spirit, even if they can't be here in person."

Soon Sophie arrived and greeted the family. When the time for public visitation neared, Grace quietly let Jennifer and Jack know that people were beginning to arrive. She asked if they were ready to allow guests to enter the room.

Jennifer looked at Jack. "Are we ready?" she said.

"If and when you are," Sophie offered, "it might help to have a transition. I brought the reading we talked about. I was thinking you might like me to read it aloud with just your family before everyone else starts arriving."

So a few minutes later Sophie read the poem "All is Well" while Carol Williams' children and grandchildren stood and held hands, heads bowed, in a semi-circle around the open side of her casket, one of her favorite songs playing quietly in the background. There was more hugging and crying, and when Jennifer let Grace know they were ready, the doors were opened.

Right away guests began to trickle in, and Jennifer and Jack couldn't believe who showed up—aunts and uncles, distant cousins, Carol's old university colleagues and bowling league members, the gardening community, fellow hospice volunteers as well as the hospice team who'd cared for Carol, old neighbors and recent neighbors, Jack and Jennifer's childhood friends and their current friends and coworkers. Even some of Jack and Jennifer's children's friends came.

The afternoon and evening were a blur of hugs and tears and laughter, of shared memories both familiar and new, of approaching Carol's body and looking down on her with love and sadness, of sneaking away for a few minutes now and then to breathe and regroup, of telling and retelling stories of her life and her death, of mourning together—all with Carol herself the undeniable, present focus of the experience.

At the close of the evening visiting hours, Carol Williams' family sat in the visitation room chairs. Jennifer was holding the guest book in her lap and counting how many guests they'd received.

"More than a hundred people came!" she marveled. "I'm drained, but what a memorable day."

Once again Grace remained, still and patient, at the back of the room. The family would soon leave for the night, but Grace did not want to make the slightest move to rush them, even though she was tired. She understood that Jennifer and Jack would let her know when they were ready to go. In the meantime, every additional moment they spent together at Carol Williams' side was a moment they needed to truly acknowledge the reality of the death, embrace the pain of the loss, and support one another. Grace felt privileged to be able to give them the gift of this time. She also thought back to the days when the family would have sat vigil all day and all night at the side of their loved one who died—the "wake" in "awake." Grace sometimes thought that the modern-day equivalent gave the family short shrift, but she would do everything in her power to protect what little time they did have left with their loved one who died.

When Jennifer cued Grace that they were ready to go, the Williams family gathered once more around the casket, and Sophie read a closing reading.

Jennifer leaned down to kiss her mother. "I'll see you tomorrow,

Mom," she whispered. Other family members followed suit, saying "Goodnight" and "I love you, Grammy" to Carol's body. Grace knew that what the family was really doing was saying hello to the new reality of life without the physical presence of their precious mother and grandmother. They were saying hello to their grief and to accepting support from each other and their community. There would be many more hellos on the long pathway to good-bye.

After Grace had seen everyone out of the Knight & Day building and locked the doors, she decided to walk to her nearby apartment rather than drive. The summer night was balmy. A breeze rustled the trees, and the dusky last rays of the sun washed the world in gold. As Grace walked and unwound, she thought back on all the special moments that Jennifer, Jack, and their families had already had throughout the funeral planning process and the visitation. Grace knew that she was doing the most meaningful work she could ever imagine. And tomorrow's fantastic funeral for Carol Williams would be a testament to that.

QUESTIONS FOR REFLECTION:

1. What is your overall impression of Grace's and Sophie's handling of Carol Williams' visitation?

2. How does your experience with visitations (both as a funeral director and an attendee) compare to Carol Williams' visitation?

3. Do you think flower arrangements at visitations and funerals are meaningful? Why or why not? What has been your experience in talking to families about funeral flowers?

4. Notice the elements of ritual that Grace and Sophie added to this visitation. The photos, the memorabilia display, the personalized music, the flowers, the opening and closing readings—in what ways did these touches affect the family and guests who spent time at the visitation?

5. How do you talk to families about visitation at the arrangement conference, especially families who are predisposed to skip visitation?

CHAPTER 9

The Funeral

On the morning of Carol Williams' funeral, Sam and John Knight arrived at First Episcopal Church well before the ceremony was scheduled to begin. The sun shone brightly, and the leaves of the towering oak tree in the churchyard cast a lovely dappled shade around the sanctuary's main entrance. John parked Knight & Day's coach there and stayed with Mrs. Williams while Sam entered the church to check in with Reverend Zimmerman and to see if Jennifer Jones, her brother, Jack Williams, and their families had yet arrived.

As Sam stepped through the sanctuary to the church offices, he noted the lack of flower arrangements. The Williams family had requested gifts to the community gardens in lieu of flowers and would appreciate the several hundred dollars that had already accumulated. Sam could hear the organist warming up. He hummed along to "A Mighty Fortress Is Our God" until he neared the Williams family, who had gathered in the library. Beside them stood Reverend Zimmerman, dressed in his white vestments. He held *The Book of Common Prayer* open in his one hand and the funeral bulletin in the other, reviewing the order of service so that all the family members knew what to expect and what they were to do. Reverend Zimmerman was a kind, soft-spoken man, but Sam noticed that the Williams family seemed subdued and quiet. This was to be expected.

Soon Reverend Zimmerman excused himself, and Sam spoke to Jennifer and Jack. "Everything is set on my end," he assured them. "And it looks like all is in order here. Is there anything you need my help with or are concerned about?"

"I don't think so," Jennifer sighed. "I think we're just tired."

"I understand," Sam said. "This is a difficult and draining time."

Grace stood next to Carol Williams' open casket inside the community garden's education building. She and the funeral celebrant, Sophie Blue, had just finished making sure everything was set up nicely for the outdoor funeral—a large white awning in case of rain, seating for a hundred, a microphone and speakers, a special projector and large screen for outdoor daytime use, a portable lectern, and a welcome table arranged with an oversized guest book, bright pink programs, a gardening basket filled with smooth stones, a cupful of fine-tip black Sharpies, and a simple vase of pink dahlias.

Surrounding the tent were the community garden's lush beds of annuals—including more dahlias—and a large flagstone fountain gently bubbling into the reservoir at its base. Through the window, Grace could see reflections of the summer sun and blue skies shimmering on the water's surface.

Leaving Sophie with Carol Williams' body, Grace walked out of the air-conditioned building and over to the garden's entrance. The gardens were closed to the general public for the morning, and the gardens director had assured Grace that their staff at the entrance booth would tactfully turn away visitors who were not there for the funeral while making funeral guests feel welcome.

Soon Jennifer and Jack and their families arrived. Grace greeted them with a hug and let them know that their mother was inside. After some private family time with Carol, Grace would invite guests for the last hour of visitation before the ceremony began.

"Oh, Mom," whispered Jennifer as she covered her mother's hands with her own. "It's the most beautiful day, and we're all here together in this beautiful place. For you. Because of you. Because we love you."

Jack put his arm around his sister while she cried. Jennifer and Jack's

"Is the casket here?" Jack asked.

"Yes," said Sam. "The coach is parked near the sanctuary. Are the pallbearers here? We'll have them place the casket on the church truck—which is like a special gurney—and wheel it into the back of the sanctuary. Then when the service starts, the deacon, who will be carrying a paschal candle, and the minister will lead the procession up the aisle. I will be in charge of rolling the casket behind them."

Sam then led the six black-suited pallbearers to the coach, and they brought Mrs. Williams into the sanctuary. Sam draped the church's white funeral pall over the dark walnut casket. Guests began to trickle in and were seated by ushers. Soon the family was seated in the front two pews, the organist launched into "Lift High the Cross," the congregation stood, and the deacon, the cross-bearer, and Reverend Zimmerman began the procession, followed by the Sam and the palled casket.

Reverend Zimmerman stood in the chancel and intoned the anthem and then prayers. As he spoke, Sam, seated in the back pew, made a quick headcount of the guests. Other than the family, there were about forty in attendance—an average turnout for an elderly person, especially one whose spouse had died years ago.

The congregation stood to sing hymns from the hymnal a couple of times and bowed their heads in prayer when appropriate. Jennifer Jones' son read Psalm 23, and Jack's daughter read Revelations 7. Reverend Zimmerman read the Gospel and then mounted the pulpit to deliver the eulogy.

"While I am sorry to say I did not have the privilege of knowing Carol Williams, I have learned this week that she lived a full children and spouses joined them, and they formed a Williams' family hug.

The sound system played music softly in the background as guests began to arrive. Some had come to the visitation the day before; some hadn't. Among those who had, Grace noticed a relative sense of ease. They approached Carol Williams' body with familiarity, even fondness. These guests, in turn, put the new guests at ease. As more and more people flowed in, Grace found herself counting heads. Were there enough chairs? Yes, but barely.

When it was time for the ceremony to begin, Grace ushered the family and guests outside. Sophie was waiting for them at the welcome table, and she gave each guest a program and a stone, asking them to use a Sharpie to write a short memory, phrase, or message on it at some point during the ceremony. The stones would be collected later.

Sophie gave the family and guests a minute to settle in and appreciate the beautiful surroundings. She went to the microphone and introduced herself. She took a moment to orient the guests to the program and what they could expect over the next hour.

Then Sophie stepped to the side, and Carol Williams' youngest granddaughter perched on the stool in front of the microphone. As she strummed and sang "The Prettiest Flowers," the pallbearers carried the simple pine casket up the aisle and placed it on the bier, near the lectern. As they had planned, Grace reopened the casket lid so that everyone could focus on the person they had gathered to mourn.

The funeral ceremony for Carol Williams proceeded with similar personalization, intimacy, and tenderness. Other friends and family members had been invited to do short readings—from ancient mystic poets, contemporary journalists, and the Bible. Interspersed with life and was beloved by many," said the minister. He proceeded to summarize her life as it was recounted in the obituary. He shared several brief anecdotes about Carol's life as a mother and grandmother, then spent the remainder of the eulogy celebrating her resurrection from the dead and giving praise to God and Jesus Christ for their gift of salvation.

Throughout the eulogy, Jennifer dabbed at her eyes with tissues. Jack remained stoic. The brief mentions of Carol's personal life, however, gave rise to several bursts of laughter among the family and guests. Sam was glad to see them engaged.

At the end of the short service, Sam directed the pallbearers to carry the casket back down the aisle and out to the waiting coach and John Knight. Since there would be no committal ceremony, John would drive the casket back to Knight & Day, where it would stay until Monday. On Monday a funeral home staff member would take Carol Williams to the cemetery, and the cemetery crew would see to her burial. Sam had made the funeral as easy as possible for Jennifer and Jack, just as he'd promised.

Sam met the Williams family at the back of the church and led them into the reception hall. He directed them to form a receiving line so that the guests would be able to greet each of them and vice versa.

"Glad that's over," Sam overheard Jack mutter to his sister.

"I just feel so numb," Jennifer replied.

"That's really normal," said Sam, looking her in the eye and offering a supportive smile. "People often feel shock and numbness for a number of days."

the readings were more musical selections, including John Denver's "Poems, Prayers, and Promises" and "In the Garden." Sophie started the eulogy then passed it off to Jack, who offered such uncharacteristically heartfelt sentiments that everyone was in tears. Jack was followed by one of his mother's longtime journalism department colleagues; his wry, back-in-the-day observations provided some levity. Finally, guests were invited to raise their hands, if they wanted to, and when they were called on, to stand and share what they'd written on their stone and why. This audience participation portion proved contagious, and many, many people ended up eulogizing Carol Williams in community fashion.

Following the eulogy was the tribute video, for which many family members had contributed photos and video clips. Carol's grandson had compiled the images and set them to music. On the screen next to eighty-two-year-old Carol in her casket, the guests watched Carol grow from a cherubic baby to a sassy teenager to a bride to a young mother. They smiled and wiped away more tears as on the screen Carol taught journalism classes, gardened, danced with her husband, cooked Christmas dinner, gardened, bowled, became a grandmother, and gardened some more. They watched Carol Williams' life flash before their eyes. They bore witness to the unique life that was lived and the special person she was.

After the tribute video, Sophie led a final prayer then invited everyone to participate in the procession to Collinsville Cemetery, where they would close with a brief yet meaningful committal ceremony. On their way out, the guests placed their handwritten stones in a glass bowl designated for that purpose. The stones would be a meaningful keepsake for the family and could later be added to one of their gardens or placed at the base of a tree planted in Carol Williams' memory.

As the guests filed into the reception hall to offer their condolences to the family and share in a simple meal, which the church bereavement committee had provided and would be serving, Sam stood back and observed. The solemn decorum of the ceremony was giving way to relaxed hugs, tears, laughter, and conversation. The Williams family had made it through.

The family encircled Carol Williams one final time. They held hands and were invited to speak any last words before the casket was closed, though, Sophie gently pointed out, they could always and forever talk to their mother and grandmother at the cemetery or in their hearts. The Williams family spoke of their love and said their good-byes. Some kissed Carol or gripped her hand before walking away.

Finally, Grace stood with Jennifer and Jack alone at the casket and invited them to close the lid when they were ready. It didn't take long. By now, the siblings had spent many hours in the presence of their mother's precious dead body, and they knew it was time. It was time to take her to the cemetery. It was time to lower her into her grave, beside their father. It was time to start making the transition from life before the death to life after the death.

Jennifer and Jack gave Grace a gentle embrace before walking to their waiting cars with arms linked and hearts opened wide. They realized then that this death and this funeral was transforming them. In some ways, they felt more genuinely alive than they ever had before.

As Grace watched them walk away, she smiled wistfully and nodded to herself. She knew what a difference that all her efforts, along with those of the funeral celebrant, had made to this family.

QUESTIONS FOR REFLECTION:

1. This is the big day! Before you read this chapter, how did you expect each funeral service to go? In what ways did they turn out different from your expectations?

2. Like any funeral, a church funeral can be generic and empty, or it can be richly personalized and meaningful to the family. In what ways does the church funeral seem to miss the mark for Carol Williams' family? Are there any ways in which it worked for them?

3. What do you think about holding funerals at unusual locations? Do you have any experience arranging or attending such funerals? Where were they, and how did they turn out?

4. Which little touches do you think made the biggest difference in Grace's version of Carol Williams' funeral, and why?

5. If you could add one or change one thing to enhance Sam's version of Carol Williams' funeral, what would it be?

6. Sam and the funeral celebrant (the minister) did not work together on the funeral service itself. Grace and Sophie, on the other hand, worked as a team on their funeral service. What are the results of this difference?

CHAPTER 10

The Committal

GRACE GATEKEEPER

(Note: In this book's alternate reality, under Sam Standard's direction, the decision was made to have no committal service for Carol Williams and so will not be covered here.)

Carol Williams' casket rode to Collinsville Cemetery not in Knight & Day's funeral coach but instead in the back of a restored 1940 Studebaker pick-up, which belonged to Carol's son, Jack. The truck was nearly as old as Carol, and she always said it reminded her of her childhood. She had never particularly cared about cars, but when Jack's vintage-car hobby had led him to the Studebaker a number of years back, Carol had fallen in love.

The procession from the community gardens to the cemetery was led by a police escort and took the family and guests down Collinsville's main street. Grace rode with Jack and his daughter in the Studebaker. As they slowly moved along, Grace watched the people on the sidewalks and in the cars that weren't part of the cortège. Many seemed curious about the procession, looking up from their phones and bustle to respectfully acknowledge the reality and solemnity of the death of a member of their community.

At the cemetery, the pallbearers carried the casket to the waiting lowering device, at the open grave. The celebrant, Sophie Blue, instructed the family to sit in the section of chairs nearest the grave and waited for the rest of the guests to park and assemble.

The sun continued to shine, though the cemetery's tall, old trees provided a pleasant mix of shade and dappled light. The grass fairly glowed with the green of June, and the snowball bushes behind the Williams' headstone bloomed lushly. Several young children were among those in attendance, and their parents followed after them as they scampered gleefully among the nearby headstones.

Once everyone had gathered, Sophie called them to attention,

A TALE OF TWO FUNERALS

announcing that they were there to commit Carol Williams to her final resting place beside her beloved husband, Nathan. Sophie continued with a brief reiteration of Carol's qualities that had been so clearly and personally emphasized throughout the preceding funeral ceremony. She had lived a full life complete with many friendships, career and volunteer relationships, and familial love. She had experienced great joy, and she had fostered joy in those around her. She would be sorely and particularly missed.

Then Sophie read aloud a poem:

> FINDING YOU IN BEAUTY
> — *Author unknown*
>
> The rays of light filtered through
> The sentinels of trees this morning.
> I sat in the garden and contemplated.
> The serenity and beauty
> Of my feelings and surroundings
> Completely captivated me.
> I thought of you.
> I discovered you tucked away
> In the shadows of the trees,
> Then rediscovered you
> In the smiles of the flowers
> As the sun penetrated their petals,
> In the rhythm of the leaves
> Falling in the garden,
> In the freedom of the birds
> As they fly searching, as you do.
> I'm very happy to have found you.
> Now you will never leave me,
> For I will always find you in the beauty of life.

Finally, Sophie thanked everyone for their presence and support on this difficult day and reminded them that the family hoped they would also come to the luncheon that would immediately follow.

Grace invited first the family, then others, to place a single dahlia and a handful of soft, dark soil atop Carol Williams' casket as it was slowly lowered into the ground. Next Jennifer stepped forward holding a small gift box.

"My mom loved gardens as well as the butterflies that visit them," she said. "Today, butterflies to me represent not only the beauty and fleeting nature of our human lives, but also the possibility of what comes next. I believe that Mom's soul is now flying free."

Jennifer removed the box's lid, and dozens of painted lady butterflies lifted into the air and winged up and away. The crowd oohed with wonder then spontaneously broke into gentle applause.

As the mourners left the gravesite in twos and threes, Carol's neighbor played "Somewhere Over the Rainbow" on her ukulele. People stopped to talk to one another. There were more tears—and even more hugs.

Jack and Jennifer were the last to leave their mother's side. While Grace stood a distance away, the siblings gazed down at the casket, now deep inside the earth, ready to be covered over by the cemetery staff.

"I'm pretty sure Mom liked the ride in the Studebaker," Jack said. "When she told us she didn't want us to go to any trouble for her funeral, she wasn't considering the Studebaker." He lifted one eyebrow and smiled.

Jennifer looped her arm through her brother's. "Are you kidding me? She loved it!" Jennifer said. "And the gardens and the music and all the stories and the butterflies—I just feel like she was so *here* today, you know?"

"I didn't know funerals could be like this," Jack said. "I'm glad you talked me into it. You always were the smart one. Thanks."

"Thanks for being open to it," Jennifer said. "I guess we'd better get going to the reception. You know what's weird? I'm actually kind of hungry!"

After a moment of silence, Jack whispered, "Bye, Mom. We love you."

Jennifer was too consumed by tears to speak, but she blew her mother a kiss as they walked away.

QUESTIONS FOR REFLECTION:

1. What is your opinion about funeral processions from the service location to the cemetery? What do families generally think about processions?

2. How do you feel about graveside committal ceremonies? What are some of your key experiences with them?

3. During the arrangement conference, Grace taught Jennifer and Jack that the committal ceremony provides essential closure to the entire funeral process. Without it, the family does not bear witness to the burial (or scattering) of someone they love. How well do you feel Carol Williams' committal provided that sense of an ending to the funeral process?

4. In Sam Standard's reality, which lacked a procession and a committal, do you think the family is missing anything significant? Why or why not?

CHAPTER 11

The Gathering

Sam directed Jack, Jennifer, and their families to form a receiving line in the parish hall of First Episcopal Church. In this manner Carol Williams' family greeted each of the funeral guests, who were then invited to help themselves to the sandwich buffet luncheon and take a seat at the hall's round tables.

The ritual of the receiving line created a welcome structure for this final phase of the funeral. While Jack and Jennifer felt the fatigue of the last several days and of now speaking to each guest individually, they also felt the genuine love and concern of each person they greeted.

After all the guests had been received, Reverend Zimmerman led the group in a blessing. Then Jack, Jennifer, and their family members were free to go their separate ways to eat and chat more informally among themselves and with the relatives, former neighbors, church members, and others who had come to pay their respects.

Jack was surprised to see his cousins—Carol's nephews—who lived several hours away. He enjoyed hearing their memories of "Aunt Carol" and catching up with their lives.

Several of Jennifer's coworkers were there, and she appreciated their hugs and their listening ears as she updated them on what had happened. She was glad to know that when she returned to work the following week, her colleagues would understand her ongoing grief and slowly help her get back into the groove of living.

As Carol's family mixed and mingled, the church bereavement committee ladies made sure the meats, cheeses, rolls, condiments, dessert bars, coffee, and lemonade were replenished as necessary and that guests could find the restrooms and

By the time Jennifer and Jack arrived back at the community garden's education building for the catered luncheon, the hall was already abuzz with conversation and laughter.

Just as it had at the visitation, Carol's favorite music played in the background, and the guests carried clear plastic cups fizzing with Carol's famous pink rhubarb punch.

While Grace set up a table with the photos and memorabilia of Carol's life that had also been on display at the visitation, the celebrant, Sophie Blue, stepped to the microphone to call the gathering to order. The crowd quieted.

"Thank you all for taking more time from your busy day to join in a meal with Carol's family," she said. "It matters that you're here. It matters that we come together when someone we care about dies. It matters that we honor a unique and precious life that was lived and that touched so many. This reception is a time for sharing memories and stories, for reconnecting with close friends as well as people we may not have been in touch with for some time. It's a time for mourning together and for supporting one another in our continued living.

"In lieu of a formal receiving line," Sophie added, "we ask that you find a moment to say hello and offer your condolences to Jennifer, Jack, and their family members at any time before you leave. We're going to open the buffet line in a moment, and you're welcome to get some food whenever you'd like. That delicious smell that's been making us all so hungry is from Carol's favorite barbecue restaurant. We're so glad to have them catering our garden picnic today.

"But first let's share a moment of silence. I invite you to close your eyes and picture Carol in your favorite memory of her—or, if you didn't know Carol personally but are here to support her family, then your favorite anything else they needed.

The small gathering drew to a natural close about an hour and a half after the funeral service had ended. Guests said good-bye to Jennifer and Jack, and the large room began to grow quieter and quieter. Then Jennifer and Jack's families left with plans to gather again at Jennifer's house for an informal dinner that evening. Soon just Jennifer, Jack, the minister, and Sam Standard remained.

Sam gave Jennifer the guest book and an understanding smile. "It was a nice ceremony," he said. "I heard a number of the guests saying so."

"Not a bad turnout, right?" asked Jack. His uncertain expression sought validation.

"A good turnout," agreed Reverend Zimmerman. "Many people cared about your mother and your family."

"Thank you so much for everything," Jennifer said to the minister and to Sam. "It was a hard week, but both of you made it easier." She gave each of them a hug then turned to her brother. "What now?" she asked.

Jack shrugged. "I guess now we head over to your house and put our feet up."

"I'm thinking pajamas," Jennifer said, and everyone laughed.

"I'll be in touch next week about any final details," Sam said. "And remember, call me any time if you have any other questions."

Before leaving the church, Jennifer made sure to thank the women who had handled the luncheon. She stopped at the restroom, noting her drawn face in the mirror. Then she and Jack memory of your own mother."

When Sophie ended the minute of silence, tears were flowing freely again, and the reception-goers began to hug one another and spontaneously share the memories they had just privately visited in their thoughts.

As the reception went on, Jennifer and Jack heard dozens of stories about Carol they'd never heard before. It seemed like everyone was in a storytelling mood and was eager to share from their personal treasure trove of memories.

Long-lost cousins, old neighbors and teachers, Carol's former university colleagues, fellow gardeners, Jennifer and Jack's childhood friends—more people than Carol's family had dreamed possible were there to affirm that Carol's life had intersected in important ways with theirs. There was so much love and energy in the space that it was full to bursting—just like Jennifer and Jack's own hearts.

Grace stood back and watched it all unfold. She smiled to herself, understanding that people want, need, and benefit from such meaningful rituals. But, she knew, making them as thoroughly meaningful as Carol Williams' requires a little extra education, empathy, planning, and courage to cultivate mourning along the way. Once those seeds have been sown, though, all you have to do is step back and watch the garden explode with vibrant life.

As the guests trickled away, Sophie gathered Jennifer, Jack, and their families for one last private prayer and group hug. Both Sophie and Grace also received their own heartfelt, individual hugs from Jennifer and Jack.

Finally Jack and Jennifer climbed into Jack's Studebaker and rode back to Jennifer's house, where the family would be meeting up for a quiet climbed into Jack's white Honda and drove off into the sunny afternoon. Jack turned the radio on, and Jennifer looked out the window.

"It's weird," Jennifer said finally. "It's weird how everything out there looks the same even though everything's different now."

"Yeah," Jack said. "I know. I still can't really believe it."

"I just feel completely...numb." Jennifer sighed and clicked the music off. The siblings drove the rest of the way home in silence.

night together.

Jack turned the radio on, and Jennifer looked out the window.

"It's weird," Jennifer said finally. "It's weird how everything out there looks different now."

"Yeah," Jack said. "I know. Life is gonna be different."

"Still, I just feel completely…blessed," Jennifer said. "It's so, so hard, knowing that Mom's gone. But at the same time, life is so precious, you know?"

"Yes," Jack said, his voice cracking even as he smiled at his sister. "Yes, it sure is."

QUESTIONS FOR REFLECTION:

1. What purposes does the gathering or reception after a funeral serve?

2. What do you notice about variations between the one reception and the other? Which special touches or differences would you say were the most effective?

3. Would you say that both receptions are fine? Why or why not?

4. At this gathering, we're starting to see how the two different funeral processes up to this point are affecting Carol Williams' family. Attendance has been different, for one thing. So is the mood in general, and Jennifer and Jack's grief in particular. What are you noticing about the disparity over what unfolds at the one reception versus the other?

CHAPTER 12

The Aftercare

Sam relaxed into the chair at his desk at Knight & Day Funeral Home. He picked up his coffee mug and took a long drink before sighing and turning his attention to the pile of paperwork. It had been a long week—and it was only Wednesday.

Sam opened Carol Williams' file. Her funeral had been last Saturday. On Monday, he'd ensured the cemetery staff had completed her burial and closed the grave. He'd arranged for the monument company to engrave Carol's death date. He'd also notified Social Security of the death and ordered death certificate copies for the family.

Sam picked up the phone and dialed Carol's daughter, Jennifer Jones.

"Do you have a minute to talk?" Sam asked, not wanting to interrupt family time.

"Yes, now's fine," Jennifer said. "Actually, the house is empty! Mostly everyone went back to their usual routines yesterday, though I still have the rest of the week off for bereavement leave. Which is good, because I'm so tired."

"I understand. That's really common," Sam said, his voice warm and understanding. "Funerals and grief are exhausting. I'm glad you have a few more days to rest up."

Sam updated Jennifer on the grave closing, headstone engraving, and paperwork details. He asked her if she had any questions or needed anything from him right now.

"I guess not," Jennifer said. "It just seems so weird that it's all over. Thanks again for everything you did."

"You're very welcome," Sam said. "I'm glad I could help. I'll

GRACE GATEKEEPER

Grace relaxed into the chair at her desk at Knight & Day Funeral Home. She picked up her chai and took a long drink before sighing and turning her attention to the pile of paperwork. It had been a long week—and it was only Wednesday.

Grace opened Carol Williams' file. Her funeral had been last Saturday. On Monday, Grace had stopped by Jennifer's house to drop off a couple of flower arrangements that hadn't yet been delivered. A few friends and family members had also been there, and the group had spent a few minutes reminiscing about their favorite moments from Carol's funeral. There were so many!

"I just can't get over how many people participated," Jennifer had summed up. "I mean, a lot of people came, either to the visitation or the funeral or both, but so many of them also shared a story or wrote down a memory. I'm flabbergasted by all the love and support."

In addition to the straggler flowers, Grace had also brought an aftercare checklist and patiently reviewed it with Jennifer and her husband. She'd answered their questions about acknowledgment cards and memorial gifts. It had also turned out they were unsure about transferring the title to Carol's old Subaru, and Grace had been able to point them in the right direction.

"I'll call you in a couple days!" Grace had called as she hopped into her own old Subaru and eased away from the curb.

Now a couple days were up, and it was time for Grace to contact Jennifer again. She picked up the phone and dialed her number.

"Oh, I'm so glad you called!" Jennifer said immediately. "Pardon the pun, but it's dead as a tomb here. Everyone's gone back to work and school. Except me—I still have the rest of the week off. And I think the grief is really hitting me."

also be mailing you a packet with some information you might find useful, like a post-funeral checklist and information on our holiday remembrance program."

"OK," Jennifer said. "I can't think about the holidays yet, but I'll share it with Jack when the time comes."

After making sure Jennifer knew she could call him if she had any questions, Sam wrapped up the phone call then immediately set to writing Jennifer and her brother, Jack, a handwritten note of condolence as well as thanks for entrusting Knight & Day with their mother's arrangements.

Sam placed the note in a larger envelope together with a few handouts and brochures then stood to walk the packet to the receptionist's desk.

In the hallway, Sam passed John Knight.

"I heard Carol Williams' funeral went well," John said. "Good attendance for an elderly person."

"Yes, it went smoothly," Sam said. "Of course, Carol hadn't wanted her children to go to any trouble, so it's good we had a ceremony at all. I made things as easy for them as possible."

"Well, good work," said John, clapping a hand on Sam's shoulder.

"Thanks," said Sam, and his step grew a little peppier as he finished walking the aftercare packet to the receptionist for mailing.

Sam returned to his office and dug into the rest of his paperwork with renewed energy. Maybe he'd even go for a walk at

So Grace actively listened for a bit as Jennifer shared her current thoughts and feelings about her mother's death. As a funeral director, Grace was busy, but she also knew that taking ten minutes to support a grieving family member was time well spent. After all, that's what funeral homes were for.

When the timing was appropriate, Grace let Jennifer know about the grief resources available through Knight & Day, such as articles on their website and their holiday program, as well as community resources such as support groups and counselors. She also recommended a couple of excellent books.

"I'll drop off all this information at your house next week so you'll have it in writing when you're ready to look it over," Grace said. "I know it's a lot to take in right now."

Grace also told Jennifer that she'd arranged for the monument company to engrave Carol's death date on her headstone, and she'd notified Social Security of the death and ordered death certificate copies for the family.

Finally, Grace asked Jennifer for her permission to share photos from Carol Williams' funeral on the funeral home's Facebook page.

"It was such a beautiful day, and I got some lovely shots of the gardens, the flowers, the musicians playing, the Studebaker, the food, people talking and sharing memories…," Grace said. "I can tag you, so your friends and family will have access to the photos. And don't worry—I won't post anything that's not appropriate."

"Oh I would love to see photos!" Jennifer said. "I never thought about funeral pictures before, but it really was a remarkable experience. I'll be glad to have photos to remember it by. Thank you so much. I can't tell you how grateful we all are for the work you and Sophie did."

lunch and pop in to visit his mother before this afternoon's arrangement conference. Sam liked helping people. He really did.

"It was my pleasure," said Grace. "I'll call you early next week to find a time for me to drop off the information packet. Maybe we can have a cup of coffee, too? In the meantime, just call if you need anything."

Grace put together an envelope of handouts and brochures for Carol Williams' family and, after adding a handwritten note of condolence and thanks, placed it in her tickler file. She heard a knock at her door and turned to see John Knight.

"Got a minute?" John said as he stepped into the room and took a chair. "I just got off the phone with Carol Williams' daughter. She called to tell me how pleased they were with all the special arrangements and what superstars you and Sophie Blue are."

"Oh, that's so nice!" Grace said. "It really was a fantastic funeral. Sophie and I worked hard to educate Jennifer and her brother, Jack, about all of their options and why each element can be so helpful. They ended up with a really complete, loving tribute that touched a lot of people."

"Well, exceptional work," said John. "Really exceptional. I was wondering if you'd do a staff training on Carol's funeral...like a case study? We could bring in Sophie, too. Our whole team would benefit from learning how you do things. We're a good funeral home already, but I'd like us to be even better. You're the key to that."

"Sure!" said Grace, blushing a little. "How about at our staff meeting next week?"

Grace dug into the rest of her paperwork with renewed energy. Maybe she'd even go for a walk at lunch and pop in to her favorite thrift shop before this afternoon's arrangement conference. Grace liked helping people mourn well so they could go on to live and love well again. She really did.

QUESTIONS FOR REFLECTION:

1. You may have noticed that Sam is good at affirming that Jennifer and Jack's feelings are normal. Do you think this helps them? Why or why not?

2. Grace squeezes in a couple additional visits to Jennifer's house after the funeral is over. Why do you think she does that? Is that realistic? How much of a difference do you think it makes to the family's loyalty to Knight & Day but also, more importantly, to their healing?

3. Sam and Grace are both empathetic. But while Sam is task-oriented, Grace is mourning-oriented. How do you see those differences in their focuses playing out throughout this book?

4. What is your experience with funerals and social media? In what ways can it be used effectively, and in what ways is it not appropriate?

5. Why do funeral homes exist? What do you think is Sam's answer to that, and what is Grace's? What do *you* think?

6. If you could say one thing each to Sam and Grace about the funerals they arranged for Carol Williams, what would you say?

Epilogue

Jennifer Jones pushed her shopping cart through the produce section of her favorite grocery store. As she passed the display of fall apples and caught their scent, she thought of her mother, Carol Williams, who had died three months before.

Carol's favorite variety of apple had always been Yellow Delicious. She even had a Yellow Delicious tree growing in the garden of her home, which had been sold a couple of weeks ago. Another transition; another loss.

Jennifer stopped. She plucked a Yellow Delicious from the bin and lifted it to her nose. Tears welled. "Miss you, Mom," she murmured.

From the other side of the apple table, a woman about her own age caught Jennifer's eye. "Oh, hello!" the woman said. "Aren't you Carol Williams' daughter? I worked with your mother at the university a long time ago, when I was first starting and she was close to retirement. My name is Megan Satterfield."

"Yes," Jennifer responded, pasting a smile onto her face. "I'm Jennifer. Jennifer Jones."

"Well, it's nice to see you," Megan said. "I was so sorry to hear about your mother. I heard that you had a private ceremony for her. I hope it was a comfort."

Over the last several months, many people had shared this misunderstanding with Jennifer. They told her that they'd seen the obituary, but since there had been no public visitation, they assumed the funeral was just for close friends and family. Jennifer regretted the fact that her mother's funeral hadn't been as well attended at it obviously could have been. She regretted being forced to have these stilted, untimely conversations wherever she went. She regretted that her mother's funeral hadn't been more

Jennifer Jones pushed her shopping cart through the produce section of her favorite grocery store. As she passed the display of fall apples and caught their scent, she thought of her mother, Carol Williams, who had died three months before.

Carol's favorite variety of apple had been Yellow Delicious. She even had a Yellow Delicious tree growing in the garden of her home, which had been sold a couple of weeks ago. Another transition; another loss.

Jennifer stopped. She plucked a Yellow Delicious from the bin and lifted it to her nose. Tears welled. "Miss you, Mom," she murmured.

From the other side of the apple table, a woman about her own age caught Jennifer's eye. "Oh, hi!" the woman said. "You're Carol Williams' daughter! I was at the funeral. It was amazing! I worked with your mother at the university a long time ago, when I was first starting and she was close to retirement. My name is Megan Satterfield."

"Oh yes, hi!" Jennifer said. "I was just thinking about Mom. These were her favorite apples."

Megan came around the table to give Jennifer a hug. Jennifer cried a few tears as the two women reminisced about Carol as well as her remarkable funeral.

As they parted, Megan said, "I just want you to know that I will never think of funerals in quite the same way again. I've even started talking to my own parents and siblings about ceremony ideas that will help us all when the time comes. They think I'm a little crazy, but I can also tell that they're starting to understand that there are funerals—and then there are *funerals*, you know?"

"I *do* know," said Jennifer. "I didn't before, but I do now. Grace, our funeral director, and Sophie, the funeral celebrant, totally knocked it out of the park. Just ask if you ever need their contact info. And if you 'friend' me on Facebook, I'll share the funeral photos with you. You might even be in a couple of them!"

open and inclusive.

After chatting for a few seconds, Megan and Jennifer parted ways, and Jennifer continued on her usual circuit through the store. Repeatedly, though, she found herself spacing out, walking right past items on her list. Actually, she'd experienced disorientation frequently since her mother's death. She still felt numb and out of it. Tears sprang to her eyes again, but this time they were tears of frustration instead of sorrow.

In the dairy department, Jennifer stopped in front of the wall of yogurt. She stretched for her husband's favorite, but since it had been moved to the top shelf, her five-foot two-inch frame could no longer reach it.

"Let me help," said a kindly older man's voice.

"Oh thank you," Jennifer said, and she turned to look at the man. He was familiar… "Aren't you John Knight, of Knight & Day Funeral Home?" Jennifer asked. "You handled my mother's service a few months back."

"Yes, I remember," said John. "Sam Standard was your funeral director. I hope you and your family are doing as well as can be expected."

John and Jennifer exchanged pleasantries, and Jennifer mentioned that she still felt shocked, as if she was still in denial. She also told John that in retrospect, she wished her family had been more encouraged to hold a public visitation. "It's just really hard," she added, choking back a sob and giving John a little wave as she headed off for who knows where to add who knows what to her cart.

John watched Jennifer walk away. He empathized with her struggle. In his line of work, he well understood the power and

Jennifer continued on her usual circuit through the store. Along the way, she ran into several other people who knew her family, and though they hadn't attended her mother's funeral, they'd read the long, personalized obituary in the newspaper and remembered the photo of Carol in her gardening hat.

In this manner, comfortable conversations sprang up, and support was given and received. Actually, this kind of thing had been happening to Jennifer everywhere she went in the past several months. People were coming out of the woodwork to call or send a note or share their stories of her mother's life.

Even within her own family, everyone had been supporting one another more noticeably than usual. Family members, including Carol's grandchildren, were calling and texting more often than they typically did. They'd also gotten together for large family dinners several times and were already starting to talk about holiday plans. It felt good, and Jennifer knew her mother would be pleased.

To Jennifer it felt like a wellspring of love, communication, and mutual support had been opened by her mother's remarkable funeral, and now that it had been opened, it had momentum to stay open.

In the dairy department, Jennifer stopped in front of the wall of yogurt. She stretched for her husband's favorite, but since it had been moved to the top shelf, her five-foot two-inch frame could no longer reach it.

"Let me help," said a kindly older man's voice.

"Oh thank you," Jennifer said, and she turned to look at the man. He was familiar... "Aren't you John Knight, of Knight & Day Funeral Home?" Jennifer asked. "You handled my mother's service a few months back. Actually, I called you after the service to let you know what an amazing job your funeral director and celebrant did. I'm Jennifer Jones."

"Of course. I remember," said John, shaking Jennifer's outstretched hand.

necessity of grief. He and his staff did what they could to help grieving families, but now he wondered if they could do more. He wondered if the typical service Sam Standard had arranged for Carol Williams had missed the mark. He saw an emptiness in Jennifer's eyes that concerned him.

Maybe he would schedule a special staff meeting to discuss what opportunities, if any, the Knight & Day team might be missing or skipping over as they helped at-need families. In fact, he'd text himself a reminder.

As John retrieved his cell phone from his pocket, it slid from his hand and plopped onto the bottom shelf of the yogurt case. He picked it out from its watery hiding place among the plastic yogurt containers and wiped it on his pants leg.

This was the second episode in recent months in which John's phone had gotten wet. The last time, it had made the screen's backlighting go green. Now as he dried it off, he saw that it had returned to its normal, white glow.

Little did John Knight know, but he and Knight & Day Funeral Home had just emerged from the space-time anomaly they had inhabited over the past three months. Carol Williams had two funerals. They had occurred simultaneously in parallel universes. Not only were the funerals different, but, more importantly, the mourning and healing trajectories they had created for Carol's family and friends were also vastly different.

John Knight, his funeral directors Sam Standard and Grace Gatekeeper, and Carol Williams' family will never fully understand the strange duality of what happened in these pages. Instead, we, the readers, are the fortunate recipients of the wisdom they reveal. Now it is up to us to put that wisdom into practice.

"I want you to know that after your mother's ceremony, I asked Grace and Sophie to conduct a staff training. They have so many innovative ideas to share, and now Knight & Day is starting to implement a lot of them with all the families we serve."

"That's great!" Jennifer said. "My mom's funeral was just such a…tapestry of experience, you know? A bunch of small elements, but when you wove them together, wow—did they ever create something magical and much larger than the sum of their parts."

"A tapestry. I like that," said John.

John Knight returned home from the grocery store that day and went to his foyer. He spent a number of minutes gazing at the beautiful tapestry that hung there, which he'd inherited from his great-grandparents.

The only other piece of fabric in John Knight's foyer was a simple throw rug. The rug was serviceable, he thought. It did its job, but it was nothing remarkable. It would not be passed down to his children and theirs. It would not make a transformative difference in anyone's life.

Had Knight & Day been arranging throw-rug funerals all these years when they could have been arranging tapestries? Perhaps. John Knight felt fortunate to have learned the difference.

And now that we know better, we're doing better, thought John. *We can't always convince families to create tapestries, but we can strive to educate them about the purposes and elements of funerals, and help them make choices that are good for them whenever possible. We can be advocates for authentic grief and mourning. And we can be true funeral service leaders and educators in our community.*

John Knight went to find his wife and tell her about the tapestry idea. He'd worked in funeral service for a long time, but never had he been more excited about the possibilities.

QUESTIONS FOR REFLECTION:

1. Three months after her mother's funeral, how is Jennifer doing in Sam's reality? How is she doing in Grace's reality? What does the difference have to do with the funeral?

2. In what ways is a meaningful funeral like a tapestry? In what ways is a generic, abbreviated funeral like a throw rug?

3. Why are tapestry funerals more healing for families?

4. Do you think more funeral directors need to be like Grace? Why or why not?

5. What additional training and funeral service education might be needed for more funeral directors to embrace Grace's mindset and methods?

6. What is one small thing you can do today that will help you move a step closer to creating funeral tapestries?

A Final Word

If grief is normal and necessary after the death of someone loved, and if expressing and being supported in our grief are the mechanisms through which we eventually heal, then meaningful funeral experiences are indispensable.

This is the premise of *A Tale of Two Funerals*. This is the reason I'm so passionate about authentic, elements-rich funerals—and the role of funeral directors as gatekeeper.

I believe that your work is absolutely essential. You see, we live in a time in which our culture is forgetting why we have funerals. The world's first death-free generation; a mobile, fast-paced culture; a lack of understanding of the role of pain and suffering; an obsession with always being happy and entertained; and other factors have combined to create a trend toward devaluing and even eliminating funerals.

Thank goodness for funeral directors! You are the professionals families come to when someone they love dies. You are among the few who stand between them and the increasingly traveled path of least resistance to an empty or nonexistent funeral ceremony.

In this story I've attempted to show how small differences in how you think about and carry out your job can make significant, long-lasting differences for families.

Sam Standard is a good funeral director, right? He is caring and kind. He is helpful. He is efficient. He always tries to make things as easy as possible for grieving families. Families like Sam, and he likes them.

Grace Gatekeeper, though, is a great funeral director. She sees her role not as someone who makes things as easy as possible for families at a time of death but rather someone who helps families get as much out of the funeral experience as possible. She is kind and helpful, but she is also, at times, challenging. She makes it a point to educate families every step of the way, even when they are inclined to object. She educates and presents choices, then she honors families' decisions. Families love Grace, and she loves them.

Sam and Grace arranged two very different funerals for Carol Williams. Sam's did not include a public visitation or a committal. The ceremony itself, which was handled by the church, was cookie cutter and impersonal. Grace's arrangement, on the other hand, drew on the complete array of possible elements and was highly personalized.

The funeral Sam arranged was a throw rug. The funeral Grace arranged was a tapestry.

Please note that in creating the two divergent storylines, I had to resort to some stock characters and plot points. First, I am *not* saying religious funerals are throw rugs! On the contrary, religious ceremonies can be extremely meaningful and transformative for families, but only when families feel connected to the place of worship, the celebrant, and the liturgy, and only if the ceremony also incorporates individualized elements, such as a personalized eulogy. Second, I am *not* saying that female funeral directors are better than male funeral directors. It's all about attitude and passion, not gender. And third, I realize that in real life things wouldn't have fallen as neatly into place on either side of the story. Family dynamics are often more complicated than what I had space to portray in this narrative.

But in general, I'm asking you and your funeral home to reconsider the approach you take with at-need families. Are you helping them get through the funeral, or are you helping them create a transformative funeral? Are you efficient, or are you effective? Are you glossing over, or are you educating?

You may have noticed that I've highlighted small sections of text here and there throughout the two storylines. These are the key moments that differentiate Sam's funeral direction from Grace's. After you've finished reading the story, the highlighting will allow you to go back through the chapters and skim for the important differences. You might be surprised to find that they're brief and relatively infrequent. Grace simply stops to educate about the "whys" more often and listens better for small opportunities to add value.

You are busy, I know. And a lot is being asked of you already. But I hope this story challenges you to become a great funeral director. Imagine what a difference you could make not only in the lives of grieving families, but in your community, your country, and your world. Consider creating a study group with other funeral directors to read and discuss the contents of this book. Together you can create a plan.

Godspeed. I hope we meet one day.

Why We Need Funerals Training

This motivational, information-rich seminar evolved out of a need to provide funeral professionals with an excellent learning experience focused on an in-depth understanding of the elements of meaningful funerals and how to convey value to the families you serve. In this 3-day seminar, respected educator Dr. Alan Wolfelt will explore

- The "WHY"s of the funeral

- The elements of the funeral

- What the WHYs have to do with the elements

- How to use this information to help families and transform the funeral experience for them and for your organization

Call or e-mail the Center for Loss office at (970) 226-6050 for additional information about this exciting seminar or visit: **www.centerforloss.com/bookstore/why-seminar**

Bring Dr. Wolfelt
to your community!

One of today's most respected and popular educators, Dr. Alan Wolfelt presents dozens of workshops on grief and funeral service each year to both laypeople and professional bereavement caregivers throughout Noth America. Sponsors include funeral homes, hospices, universities, churches, schools—any organization interested in providing education to community members, area professionals or staff. Presentation formats include all day workshops, breakfast or dinner presentations, keynote addresses and in-house trainings, and range from just a few participants to auditorium-sized audiences. For a free, comprehensive packet on sponsorship opportunities for Dr. Wolfelt, please call the Center for Loss at (970) 226-6050.

"I am writing to acknowledge the profound impact your two workshops have had on our city and our funeral home. We see your two workshops as a turning point in our efforts to be recognized and accepted as part of the professional caregiver community."
Funeral Director/Owner

"Thank you so much for bringing Dr. Wolfelt to our community. He is a wonderful speaker and helped all of us who were fortunate to attend this program."
Bereaved Person

"I am inspired by Dr. Wolfelt's concept of companioning vs. treating the bereaved. Your funeral home is to be commended for making this workshop possible."
Hospice Staff Member

Seminars for
Bereavement Caregivers

Have you heard about the great courses for bereavement caregivers taught by Dr. Wolfelt at the Center for Loss in Fort Collins, Colorado?

He offers four-day seminars on the following topics:

- Comprehensive Bereavement Skills Training

- Counseling Skills Fundamentals

- Exploring the Spiritual Dimensions of Death, Grief and Mourning

- The Depression of Grief

- PTSD: Companioning the Traumatized Griever

- Exploring the Shadow of the Ghosts of Grief

- Exploring the Paradoxes of Mourning: Implications for Caregivers

- Suicide Grief: Companioning the Mourner

- Helping Children and Adolescents Cope with Grief

- Support Group Facilitator Training

- Understanding and Responding to Complicated Mourning

An accredited certification in Death and Grief studies is also available.

For more information, please visit our website (www.centerforloss.com) or call us at (970) 226-6050 to request a course catalog.

Creating Meaningful Funeral Experiences: A Guide for Caregivers

This revised, updated version of Dr. Wolfelt's groundbreaking *Creating Meaningful Funeral Ceremonies* includes current statistics as well as an

introduction to the concept of funerals not just as ceremonies, but as experiences. The book explores the ways in which personalized funerals transform mourners. It also reviews qualities in caregivers that make them effective funeral planners and provides practical ideas for creating authentic, personalized and meaningful funeral experiences.

ISBN 1-879651-38-6 • 80 pages • softcover
$12.95

ALL DR. WOLFELT'S PUBLICATIONS CAN BE ORDERED BY MAIL FROM:
Companion Press | 3735 Broken Bow Road | Fort Collins, CO 80526
(970) 226-6050 | www.centerforloss.com

Creating Meaningful Funeral Ceremonies: A Guide for Families

This compassionate, friendly workbook affirms the importance of the personalized funeral ritual and helps families create a ceremony that will be

both healing and meaningful for years to come. Designed to complement the clergy and funeral director's role in the funeral planning process, *A Guide for Families* walks readers through the many decisions they will make at the time of a death.

ISBN 1-879651-20-3 • 80 pages • softcover
$12.95

SPECIAL SET PRICE: Order both *Creating Meaningful Ceremonies* books for more than 20% off! *Creating Meaningful Funeral Ceremonies* set - $20.00

ALL DR. WOLFELT'S PUBLICATIONS CAN BE ORDERED BY MAIL FROM:
Companion Press | 3735 Broken Bow Road | Fort Collins, CO 80526
(970) 226-6050 | www.centerforloss.com

Afterwords...Helping You Heal

A compassionate, affordable aftercare packet for hospices & funeral homes

The distillation of many of Dr.Wolfelt's key teachings, Afterwords offers compassionate, empowering messages about grief and healing to the newly

bereaved. Section headings include The Grief Journey, Myths About Grief, Helping Yourself Heal, a Directory of Bereavement Organizations and Support Groups (including websites), a Selected Reading List and the Mourner's Bill of Rights.

Unlike similar packets, Afterwords does not promote its publisher (in this case Companion Press), but instead is designed to highlight your organization's role in aftercare delivery. Our name only

appears in a brief "about the author" blurb within the text.

Afterwords is an easy-to-use, high quality aftercare packet for hospices, hospitals and funeral homes. And Afterwords is affordable, too. Send for the sample packet for details.

$10.00 (sample packet and ordering information; $10 applied to first order)